THE
FISKE GUIDE
TO

GETTING INTO
THE
RIGHT COLLEGE

THE
FISKE GUIDE
TO
GETTING INTO THE RIGHT COLLEGE

The Complete Guide to Everything You Need to Know to Get into and Pay for College

Edward B. Fiske
with Bruce G. Hammond

T I M E S 𝕿 B O O K S

R A N D O M   H O U S E

All rights reserved under International and Pan-American Copyright Conventions. Published in the United States by Times Books, a division of Random House, Inc., New York, and simultaneously in Canada by Random House of Canada, Limited, Toronto.

ISBN 0-8129-2779-6

Library of Congress Cataloging-in-Publication data is available.

Random House website address: http://www.randomhouse.com/
Manufactured in the United States of America

9 8 7 6 5 4 3 2

First Edition

To our parents

CONTENTS

PART ONE: FINDING THE RIGHT COLLEGE

PART TWO: GETTING IN

PART THREE: PAYING THE BILL

PART FOUR: A TIME TO REFLECT

PART ONE

FINDING THE RIGHT COLLEGE

The Search Begins

(or, What to Do When You Don't Have a Clue)

The college advising office in your high school can be a pretty intimidating place, especially on your first visit. An eerie silence pervades the room. As you cross the threshold and survey the scene, your eye catches the twelfth-grade boy who used to flick spitballs into your hair from the back of the bus when you were in middle school. He's still wearing the same flea-bitten Metallica T-shirt, but now his nose is buried in a college guide as he scribbles feverishly in a spiral notebook. On the other side of the room, the girl from down the street with the doting mother and the 4.0 grade point average is staring purposefully into a computer screen, clacking the keyboard every few seconds as she calls up a new file. Suddenly, you get a sinking feeling that she and all the other kids in the room know exactly what they're doing. You're the only one who doesn't have a clue. Of course, you could always ask Mrs. Stonebreaker for help. That is, if you don't mind the familiar glasses-on-the-end-of-the-nose routine and the icy stare that says you've just asked the stupidest question of her thirty-four-year career. You want to beat a hasty retreat and come back later—much later.

It's no wonder that beginning college applicants often get the strong urge to run away and hide. Talk about an intimidating situation! Many students have barely gotten comfortable in high school before the college search looms ominously on the horizon. Rumblings about "selective colleges" and "the job market" begin to pop up in dinner conversations and guidance-office bulletin boards. Friends who used to be party animals suddenly begin to hit the books and talk about "getting the grades for college." Relatives you haven't seen in years marvel about how much you've grown—and then want to know all about your career plans.

As if those storm clouds weren't threatening enough, there is the little matter of finding *one* college out of about 2,200 four-year schools in the nation. They come in more flavors than Baskin-Robbins or Ben and Jerry ever dreamed of making—large, small, middle-sized, rural, urban, and a thousand permutations. If colleges were ice cream, a student could sample four or five flavors and make a choice. Unfortunately, college applicants must get it right the first time or go through the same agony again when they transfer. How can you figure out what sort of college is right for you?

One place you won't find the answer is your mailbox, which, if you have checked a certain box on your PSAT or SAT exam, has become a direct pipeline to the propaganda factories of colleges coast to coast. Though the deluge of college mail can be highly entertaining, every school from Harvard to Ho Hum U. advertises a similar bill of goods. If you were confused before, try figuring out the difference between two colleges by reading the glossy view books. The scenes in their pages are always the same: eager hordes of racially diverse undergraduates thinking deep thoughts, or frolicking in perpetual spring against a backdrop of white columns and grassy lawns. Let's see now . . . College X offers "academic excellence" and "rich diversity." On the other hand, College Y offers "rich diversity" and "academic excellence." Still can't tell the difference?

Meanwhile, all the adults in your life (and a few you've never seen before) offer their two cents about where you should go to school. From your grandfather, you get the latest updates on colleges and the job market from *U.S. News & World Report.* Mom says that you can choose any school you want—as long as you stay within fifty miles of home. Even your Uncle Pete, whom you barely know, takes you under his wing and says he has the perfect college for you based on his wonderful experience in the early 1950s.

If you're confused by conflicting advice, if you're put off by college propaganda, if you're eager to get started but don't know where to begin, this book is your ticket to a successful college search. We'll take you on a guided tour of the entire process: how to find the right college for *you,* how to get in, and how to pay for it. Along the way, we'll help you focus your thoughts and figure out what you're really looking for. We'll tell you how to cut through the college-search nonsense, and then give you insider sketches of hundreds of colleges in dozens of categories. We'll reveal the secrets of the highly selective admissions game, and how you can play it to win. And finally, we'll delve into the shadowy world of college financial aid—how to get your hands on it, and how your need for it may affect your chances for admission.

Before we begin plotting strategy, let's step back for a minute and remind ourselves of what the college search is all about. Amid all the anxiety about getting in, it helps to keep the big picture in mind.

WHY COLLEGE?

That may seem like a stupid question, but there is more to the answer than meets the eye. Practicality says that people go to college to get a good job after graduation, and there is plenty of research to show that college is a sound economic investment. On the average, college graduates can expect to earn more than twice as much as those with a high school diploma over a working lifetime, and the gap is widening.

There are two schools of thought about how to get the most out of your college experience. Many educators stress the value of exposure to a broad spectrum of human knowledge. The phrase "liberal arts education" connotes learning that "liberates" the mind to think new thoughts. A liberal arts education is an introduction to the great events and ideas of the past, as well as the most recent discoveries of today. It can include history, art, astronomy, zoology, and everything in between. It doesn't prepare you for any particular job, but instead equips you with the basic skills—reading, writing, thinking—to meet any challenge that comes down the pike.

The alternative to liberal-arts education is to use college to prepare for a particular career. This approach often sacrifices a well-rounded general education in favor of material related to a particular job or subset of jobs. Some careers, such as engineering and architecture, require concentrated training beginning in the freshman year that leaves little time for smelling the roses. In today's tight job market, nervous undergraduates often feel strong pressure to "major in something practical."

In addition to its economic function, college attendance also provides a high school graduate with the first public measure of his or her academic and personal success. Admission to a "name" college is like getting an A in growing up, and comes with the presumption of future success to follow. The ego of anyone—especially a seventeen-year-old—is fragile. Who wouldn't want a stamp of approval from one of the world's most respected and recognized institutions?

With all the practical reasons to attend, let us not forget that college is also a once-in-a-lifetime experience. You can test your limits, try new things, and make some incredibly stupid mistakes—all without the respon-

---

According to the *Oxford English Dictionary,* the term "liberal arts" dates back to the fourteenth century. In those days, the "seoven ars" comprised grammar, logic, rhetoric, arithmetic, geometry, music, and astronomy.

Famous Liberal Arts Graduates

	MAJOR
Richard Chamberlain	Art
Katie Couric	American Studies
Newt Gingrich	History
Hugh Grant	English
Conan O'Brien	Literature and U.S. History
Regis Philbin	Sociology
Colin Powell	Geology
Janet Reno	Chemistry
Maria Shriver	American Studies
Gloria Steinem	Government

Source: Current Biography

sibility of having to make a living. The friendships you form will last a life-time, and so too will the memories. Decades from now, when you're rocking away the retirement years on the front porch, college will probably rank high on the list of things that made life worth living.

There is no perfect way to categorize everything a college experience can give you, but these are the basics: (1) a liberal-arts education, (2) career training, (3) a prestigious affiliation, (4) a once-in-a-lifetime experience. Which of them seems most important to you? Are there other benefits that you think are just as crucial? Don't feel pressure to answer right away, because your choice will probably dictate the shape of your college search. Most applicants will be looking for a combination of some or all, but the process of examining priorities is still useful. If (1) ranks high, you'll definitely want to look at liberal arts institutions where teaching is a high priority. Those interested in (2) should focus less on general characteristics than on the programs in their field of interest. Interest in (3) means playing the highly selective-admissions game. If (4) is a high priority, you may be the kind of person who marches to his or her own drummer, or at least the type who is less interested in high-powered academics than a healthy balance between work and play.

Only you can decide what is important in a college, but we would like to help you avoid two major pitfalls.

First, many applicants mistakenly think that prestige automatically equals academic quality. Call it the brand-name syndrome: the idea that if you haven't heard of a college, it can't be any good. Many big-name schools do deliver educational excellence, but others are overcrowded, overrated, and coasting on reputation. There are scores of comparatively little-known colleges, most of them small, that offer an education every bit as good.

But you're probably thinking, Don't all the best jobs go to Ivy League graduates? Not by a long shot. They get their share, but so do graduates of countless other schools that aren't household names. In a landmark study of colleges with the highest percentage of graduates earning a Ph.D. degree, the top finisher wasn't Harvard but Harvey Mudd College. Harvard placed thirty-seventh, behind liberal arts colleges such as Eckerd, Wabash, and Kalamazoo, which continue to produce excellent graduates with much less fanfare.

Our second pitfall is also caused by career jitters. In the name of practicality, too many students get stampeded into career preparation and lose the once-in-a-lifetime chance to get an education. If you've wanted to be an accountant since age six, don't hesitate. But if you plan to major in accounting just because you think that's where the jobs are, think again. What's the point of using your college years to prepare for a career you might not enjoy? And how are you going to know unless you sample different things? In the working world, nothing is less practical than devoting fifty or sixty hours a week to a job you don't like. That is why so many high-priced lawyers and investment bankers are quitting their jobs today. They have a few extra dollars in their pockets, but they are also miserable.

College career preparation may help you land that first job, but it may also leave you stranded there when others have moved on to bigger and better things. The Bureau of Labor Statistics says that current college graduates will go through half a dozen "careers" on average. Even for those who stay in the same industry, a liberal arts education offers the flexibility to make lateral moves on the way to the top. As any corporate president will tell you, the people who get to the executive suite are the ones who see the big picture and, more often than not, got a liberal arts education.

Despite all we have said, anyone contemplating the liberal arts should probably keep at least one eye on the job market. The grim reality is that today's college graduates face tough competition. Corporate downsizing, which began in earnest in the mid-eighties, has taken a heavy toll on the number of entry-level positions. Whereas a big bank might have recruited on more than a hundred campuses ten or twenty years ago, today that same bank may only visit a dozen or two. Things are tough all over; even the Ivy League career placement offices are running a bit scared.

So what should you do? Grab your bean counter and head for an accounting class? We think not, unless accounting happens to be your passion. Our blanket recommendation is simple: Follow your interests. And follow them. And follow them. The person who succeeds in tomorrow's job market isn't going to be the one who majors in something "practical," or for that matter the one with the highest grade point average. Rather, it will be the person who pursues an interest—any interest—wherever it may lead.

When you find an academic subject that appeals to you, talk to the professor after class. Join an extracurricular group that may have related concerns, or find out from the professor about private companies that might be doing related work. Call those companies. Intern for those companies. Take summer jobs at those companies. The students who habitually take that kind of initiative, no matter what their major, are going to be the ones who get the jobs. As one high-ranking executive at B. F. Goodrich told us, "I run a $300-million-a-year operation, and frankly, I don't care what they study. We hired someone recently because he had been head of Habitat for Humanity at the University of Florida. If a person can talk intelligently about experiences they've had, I listen."

Among other things, your college experience will give you four years to search out at least one thing that you love to do. Once you've found your passion, go after it with everything you've got. You may find that what is the most interesting is also the most practical.

In the final analysis, your college experience is about something even more important than your career: the kind of person you will one day become. In one of his final reports as President of Yale University, Kingman Brewster, Jr., described the value of a liberal arts education, and we can think of no better way to make the case than to remember his words:

The most fundamental value of a liberal education is that it makes life more interesting. This is true whether you are fetched up on a desert island or adrift in the impersonal loneliness of the urban hurly-burly. It allows you to see things which the undereducated do not see. It allows you to understand things that the untutored find incomprehensible. It allows you to think things which do not occur to the less learned. In short, it makes it less likely that you will be bored with life. It also makes it less likely that you will be a crashing bore to those whose company you keep.

2
Sizing Yourself Up

There is nothing complicated about finding a college. Put simply, the whole process is a game of matchmaking. You have interests and needs; the college has programs that meet those needs. If all goes according to plan, you'll both live happily ever after—or at least for four years.

Unfortunately, most of the players in your college search have agendas of their own. Many colleges today are more interested in making a sale than they are in making a match. Under intense competitive pressure, many won't hesitate to sell you a bill of goods if they can get their hands on your tuition dollars. Guidance counselors generally mean well, but they are often under duress from principals and trustees to steer students toward prestigious schools regardless of whether the fit is right. Your friends won't be shy with advice on where to go, but their knowledge is generally limited to a small group of hot colleges that everyone is talking about. National publications rake in millions by playing on the public's fascination with rankings, but a close look at their criteria reveals distinctions without a difference.

Before you find yourself spinning headlong in this merry-go-round, take a step back. This is your life and your college career. What are *you* looking for in a college? Think hard, and don't answer right away. Perhaps the most difficult aspect of the college application process is the self-assessment. Before you throw yourself and your life history on the mercy of college admissions officers, you need to take some time to objectively and honestly evaluate your needs, likes and dislikes, strengths and weaknesses. What do you have to offer a college? What can a college do for you?

Unlike the high school selection process, which is usually an act of fate based on your parents' property lines, income level, or religious affiliation, picking a college isn't a procedure you can brush off on dear ol' Mom and Dad. You have to take some initiative. You're the best judge of how well each school fits your personal needs and academic goals. We encourage you to view the college-selection process as the first semester in your higher education—we can think of no better hands-on seminar in research and decision making. Done right, it is a voyage of self-discovery with lessons as significant as any you'll learn in the classroom.

DEVELOP YOUR CRITERIA

One strategy is to begin the search with a personal inventory of your own strengths and weaknesses and your "wish list" for a college. This method tends to work well for compulsive list makers and other highly organized people. What sorts of things are you especially good at? Do you have a list of skills or interests that you would like to explore further? What sort of personality are you looking for in a college? Mainstream? Conservative? Offbeat? What about extracurriculars? If you are really into riding horses, you might include a strong equestrian program in your criteria. The main problem won't be thinking of qualities to look for—you could probably name dozens—but rather figuring out what criteria should play a defining role in your search.

Students with a firm career goal will want to look for a course of study that matches their needs. If you want to major in aerospace engineering, your search will be limited to schools that have the program. But outside of

---

The Humanities and the Social Sciences

If you haven't encountered these two terms in your college literature, you soon will. Along with math and the natural sciences, they make up the liberal arts. The humanities are time-honored disciplines that concern the study or expression of the human condition. They include the arts, literature, languages, history, philosophy, and religious studies. The social sciences date from the late nineteenth century, when people began to use the scientific method to analyze human culture. They include anthropology, economics, political science, psychology, and sociology.

Any good liberal arts institution will be strong in most or all of the humanities and the social sciences.

---

specialized areas like this, many applicants overestimate the importance of their anticipated major in choosing a college. If you're interested in a liberal arts field, your expected major should probably have little to do with your college selection.

A big purpose of college is to develop interests and clarify goals. Most students change their intentions regarding a major at least two or three times before graduation, and once out in the working world, they often end up in jobs bearing no relation to their academic specialty. Even those with a firm career goal may not need as much specialization as they think at the under-graduate level. If you want to be a lawyer, don't waste your time looking for something labeled "pre-law." Follow your interests, get the best liberal arts education available, and then apply to law school.

Naturally, it is never a bad idea to check out the department(s) of any likely major, and occasionally your choice of major will suggest a direction for your search. If you're really into national politics, it may make sense to look at some schools in or near Washington, D.C. If you think you're inter-ested in a relatively specialized field—say, oceanography—then be sure to look for some colleges that are a good match for you and also have programs in oceanography. But for the most part, rumors about top-ranked depart-ments in this or that should be no more than a tie-breaker between schools you like for more important reasons. There are good professors (and bad ones) in any department. Once enrolled, you'll have plenty of time to figure out who is who.

In the end, being undecided about your career path as a senior in high school is often a sign of intelligence. Don't feel bad if you have absolutely no idea what you're going to do when you "grow up." One of the reasons you'll be paying megabucks to the college of your choice is the prospect that it will open some new doors for you and expand your horizons. Instead of worrying about particular departments, try to keep the focus on "big-picture" items like "What's the academic climate?" "How big are the fresh-man classes?" "Do I like it here?" and "Are these my kind of people?"

*If you want to know more about possible fields of study, check out **The College Board Guide to 150 Popular Majors.** It offers summaries of each with information on course require-ments and career paths.*

KEEP AN OPEN MIND

The biggest mistake of beginning applicants is hyper-choosiness. At the extreme is what we call "perfect-school syndrome," which comes in two basic forms.

In one category are the applicants who refuse to consider any school that doesn't have every little thing they want in a college. If you're one who begins the process with a detailed picture of Perfect U. in mind, you may want to remember the oft-quoted advice that "two out of three ain't bad." If a college seems to have most of the qualities you seek, give it a chance. You may come to realize that some things you thought were absolutely essential are really not that important after all.

The other strain of perfect-school syndrome is the applicant who gets stuck on a "dream" school at the beginning and then won't look anywhere else. With those 2,200 four-year colleges out there, it is just a bit silly to insist that only one will meet your needs. Having a first choice is okay, but the whole purpose of the search is to consider new options and uncover new possibilities. A student who has only one dream school—especially if it is a highly selective one—could be headed for disappointment.

With apologies to Socrates, knowing thyself is easier said than done. Don't expect any quick revelations. Instead, think of it as a process that unfolds over time—kind of like the process of picking a college. Our advice? Be patient. Set priorities. Keep an open mind. Reexamine priorities. Be patient.

3
The College Universe

The most striking fact about American higher education is its diversity. Though our economy might be uncertain, our politics mired in sleaze, and our cultural life at the depths of the latest lurid talk show, the United States still has the richest assortment of colleges and universities in the world. Our 2,200 four-year schools are a smorgasbord unrivaled by any other nation on earth. American higher ed offers everything: from tiny schools where students number in the dozens to massive ones that have their own zip codes; from colleges so remote that the nearest pavement is miles away to those that are surrounded by the high-rise growth of the urban jungle; from schools where the students wear prints and pastels to those where the preferred uniform is combat boots and chains.

There are virtually as many colleges as stars in the sky, and sorting out the college universe is no easy task. To help, this chapter describes the most common varieties. Though not every school fits neatly into every category, an understanding of the trade-offs between the various types can help applicants make intelligent choices.

SIZE

One of the most important forks in the road to college happiness is the dilemma of big versus small. Do you want to attend a university, with 10,000 or 20,000 students? Or would you prefer a small college with, say, 2,000 students?

Before you can answer, we need to define some terms. Though the word "college" is used loosely to refer to a variety of institutions, strictly speaking it means a program leading to a bachelor's degree. All students enrolled in any college are "undergraduates"—that is, they have not earned a bachelor's degree. Some colleges are devoted to the liberal arts; others focus on business, engineering, architecture, or another pre-professional field. Some are freestanding institutions; others are part of a university. Colleges tend to be "small," generally enrolling 1,000 to 5,000 students.

A university is an institution that combines one or more undergraduate colleges (including one for the liberal arts) with graduate schools that give Ph.D.s, M.D.s, and other degrees. Universities vary widely in size. Most private ones have an enrollment between 5,000 and 20,000 students. Public ones range upward to behemoth Ohio State University, which tips the scales with nearly 50,000 students, including 36,000 undergraduates.

In recent years, more top applicants have been choosing universities. Bigger doesn't necessarily mean better, but it often means better-known. Leery of going to a "no-name" school, today's students are flocking to universities that have well-established programs in law, medicine, and other prestigious professions.

Aside from name recognition, there are a number of reasons why universities are attractive. Most important, they offer more courses to choose from. If you're undecided, that means more potential majors. If you're eyeing a highly specialized major, or one that requires expensive facilities, a big university may be the only place to find it. Larger schools often have the strongest departments in less prominent majors, such as anthropology or astronomy, that often get short shrift at a small school.

Outside the classroom, universities generally offer superior opportunities for people who are really good at one thing. If you want to be a newspaper reporter, a high-powered daily at a big university will probably offer much better experience than the sleepy weeklies that inhabit most small colleges. If you want to be the next Michael Jordan, the Big Ten is better than the Little Ivies. Though the competition to get the editorship or make the team is keener, those who have the talent can perform at a higher level. Socially, a large university can be welcome relief from the high school fishbowl. Many students enjoy the anonymity that comes with thousands of classmates, and the ability to move in and out of social groups without being stereotyped. The excitement of big-time sports is a strong lure, and there is also something special about that "hub of the universe" feeling in the air at great universities.

Though large universities offer unparalleled opportunities, they also put more pressure on students to take initiative. Arm yourself with a particular course of study in mind, and be ready to fight the bureaucracy. Go-getters tend to do best. Passive types generally spend too much time falling asleep in the back of huge lecture halls.

Small Colleges

We now turn to one of higher ed.'s most underappreciated resources: the small college. Many applicants seem to have a mental block about them. For starters, let's get beyond some of the myths about small schools:

Myth 1: *I'll never find a job or get into grad school if I go to a small college.* Absolutely wrong. While the names of big universities are more familiar to the general public, people in graduate school admissions and corporate recruiting are well aware of the smaller schools. "Hands-on experience" has become one of today's buzzwords, and small colleges almost always provide the best opportunities for undergraduates to do their own research, lead an organization, and so on. In a tight job market, the all-round small college doer beats the face-in-the-crowd large-university type of person every time.

Myth 2: *Small colleges aren't diverse.* In the words of M*A*S*H's Colonel Potter, "Horse hockey!" If you look at student bodies by percentage of students from various backgrounds, most small schools are every bit as diverse as the big ones. Small schools also tend to provide the best chance to sample that diversity because they aren't big enough to become segregated by special-interest groups.

Myth 3: *A small school would be too confining.* Well . . . maybe. But remember this: A small college and a small high school are not the same thing. Often, students at a small high school (say, 400 students) will be determined to attend a "big" university. They forget that a "small" college might be five or six times as large as their small high school. Do you know anyone who attends a high school of 2,500 students or more? If so, when was the last time they complained about it being "too small"?

The most compelling arguments for small colleges are academic ones. By definition, these schools have few if any graduate students, so you won't find yourself eyeball-to-eyeball with a teaching assistant in introductory math or English. Many large universities like to boast about their distinguished faculty, forgetting to mention that some do not teach undergraduates and many others have only a class or two. For many university faculty, "teaching" means two or three command performances a week in an overflowing lecture hall while graduate students conduct all the discussion sections, do all the grading, and answer all the questions.

Another small-college selling point can be summed up in one word: "involvement." Studies show that students who are active in the community perform best, and small colleges generally offer the best chance to sample, explore, and get involved in lots of different things. On paper, the large universities offer more variety, but in practice often have less. Whereas most courses offered at a small college are fair game for anyone, large universities often have strict limitations on cross-registration between divisions. If you're a business major at a big university, don't count on getting into that nifty course in the school of journalism without some fast talking, half a dozen signatures, and a lot of luck. On the other hand, small schools give you the freedom to explore varied interests. You can be a jack-of-all-trades—as you were in high school—without being elbowed aside by quasi-professionals who are on their way to fame and glory.

Socially, small colleges usually have a stronger sense of community. If claustrophobia does set in after a year or two, you can always take part of your junior year abroad—a staple of the small-college experience.

LOCATION

Perhaps the biggest difference in college admissions from a generation ago is the mobility of today's applicant. Most don't hesitate to scour all corners of the nation to find the best college. Indeed, many applicants seem to care more about *where* it is than *how good* it is.

Different regions evoke different images in the minds of high school students, often depending on where they grew up. In the age of cyberspace, college is still synonymous with a quaint New England town featuring the traditional red brick, white columns, and ivy all around. That enduring mental picture combines with the seemingly inborn cultural snobbery of the East Coast to produce millions of students who think that civilization ends at the western edge of Pennsylvania. For Midwesterners, the situation is just the opposite: a century-old cultural inferiority complex. Many applicants from those states will do anything to get the heck out, even though there are more good colleges per capita in states like Iowa, Minnesota, and Ohio than anywhere else in the nation. The West Coast fades in and out as a trendy place for college; currently, the West is out of favor because of the various woes—from earthquakes to a bad economy—that California had endured in the nineties. Among those seeking warmer weather, the South has become a popular place, especially since Southerners themselves are more likely to stay close to home.

Collective perceptions of the various regions have some practical consequences. First, most of the elite schools in the Northeast are more selective than ever. In addition, a lot of mediocre schools in the Northeast, notably Boston, are being deluged with applicants simply because they are lucky enough to be in a hot location. In the Midwest, many equally good or superior schools are much less difficult to get into, especially the fine liberal arts colleges in Ohio. In the South, the booming popularity of some schools is out of proportion to their quality. The weather may be nice and the basketball team top-notch, but students who come from far away should be prepared for culture shock.

We encourage applicants to consider schools in all parts of the nation (especially those applicants looking mainly at private colleges). Students or parents may have the impulse to say, "Nothing east of the Rockies" or "Texas is too far." But barriers like these are mainly psychological. If a student lives in Virginia, the flying time to Texas or even California isn't much more than that to Boston. Though air fares vary, they will at most add an extra $500 to $1,000 or so to the annual bill. To help attract students from far away, many colleges give out larger travel allowances in their financial-aid packages. In their eyes, applicants from other parts of the country are at a premium because they enhance campus diversity. In today's hyper-competitive admissions scene, students can significantly enhance their chances for admission if they are willing to apply to a college or university outside their home area.

Aside from regions of the country, applicants also choose whether to be in or near a city, or whether to attend college in a more rural area. In the nineties, the hottest schools tend to be in city suburbs or outskirts. These places combine access to the urban area with the safety that parents crave. The universities that are smack in the middle of cities have suffered from the growing fears of urban violence; the rural ones are called "too isolated."

Certain cities have become known as college towns. Most notable is Boston, a city that offers an unparalleled combination of safety, cultural activities, and about fifty colleges. Berkeley, California, is another mecca for the college-aged—though today an overcrowded one—and legendary college towns like Ann Arbor, Michigan; Boulder, Colorado; and Burlington, Vermont, provide wonderfully rich places for a college education.

The biggest red herring out there is the idea that "I need to be within an hour or two of a city." That is the sort of issue that, while applicants spend a lot of time thinking about it, has almost no effect on the college experience. Visit any campus and you'll hear things like "New York is only two hours away, but I can never find the time to get down there." Or, "I thought I would visit Boston a lot more than I do." More and more, colleges are becoming self-contained communities. Glitzy new student centers have everything from banks to nightclubs to fast-food joints. One college may look isolated on a map, while another appears closer to major cities, but that does not necessarily mean anything. Rural colleges realize that they are operating at a disadvantage in the eyes of some applicants, and they usually do everything in their power to bring arts, culture, and social life to their little corner of the world.

As you think about the role that location will play in your college search, here is another item to reflect on: Proximity to cities is often less important than proximity to other colleges. Potential benefits of a nearby school include cross-registration, expanded library privileges, and a fresh supply of new faces. Sometimes, students can get the best of both worlds by enrolling in a small college that has a coordinate relationship with a nearby large university. In the East, a shining example is the Massachusetts Five-College Consortium, in which four small colleges (Amherst, Hampshire, Smith, and Mount Holyoke) pool resources with the University of Massachusetts/Amherst. In the West, the Claremont Colleges have a similar setup, and dozens of other institutions in all corners of the nation have formed similar partnerships.

Finally, try to avoid rigid thinking as you consider location. Don't eliminate whole regions of the country without giving them a chance. If you grew up on the East Side of Manhattan, avoid the knee-jerk elimination of any school across the Hudson. Part of being educated is seeing how the other half lives, and college provides the perfect opportunity.

PUBLIC VS. PRIVATE

No matter what their size, American colleges and universities come in two basic types: Some are supported by the state where they are located, and hence called "public." Others are independent or affiliated with a religious group; they are called "private."

All public universities were originally founded to educate the citizens of their state, and all are subsidized by taxpayer money. These universities have traditionally had far lower tuition and less selectivity than their private counterparts, which generally serve a regional or national student body rather than residents of a particular state.

All the country's oldest colleges are private, founded when the United States consisted of the East Coast. To this day, the Northeast is still a stronghold of private colleges and universities, with few prestigious public ones. When the country expanded westward in the 1800s, public education had become a reality, and thus the state university systems in the Midwest, South, and West are much stronger.

In the 1980s, more and more top students got fed up with skyrocketing private college tuition and began to look seriously at public alternatives. In response, the public universities devoted more resources to merit scholarships and various other enticements to encourage the best students to enroll. But the 1990s have seen the rug pulled out from under the public universities. In state after state, the budget ax has fallen. Many public universities have been forced to slash their budgets and impose steep increases in tuition to keep their heads above water.

Today, public universities are still an educational bargain, though not nearly as much as they were ten or twenty years ago. On the average, in-state tuition is still less than half that of a private college, but out-of-state tuition is soaring. At some elite public universities, including the University of Michigan and the University of Vermont, out-of-staters pay as much as students at an expensive private college.

Public universities tend to be strong in professional fields like business and engineering, though some also have good programs in the liberal arts. In recent years, there have been two major growth sectors in public higher education: honors programs at the universities, and smaller liberal arts institutions that have begun to rival their private counterparts. For some general thoughts on these programs, plus descriptions of some of the best, see "Public Universities: The Honors Programs" and "Small-College Bargains" in Chapter 6.

With so many high-quality public options available, why pay an extra $50,000 for a private education? Consciously or not, most private college applicants are buying prestige. Some experts may hold their noses at such a crass reason for choosing a college, but it is interesting to note how many of these same folks themselves attended a prestigious private institution. If prestige is one of your priorities, be honest with yourself and weigh it with all your other criteria.

A more substantive benefit of private colleges, especially the elite ones, is the chance to rub shoulders with some of the best and brightest students from across the nation and around the world. There is a special intensity generated by the convergence of so many extraordinary minds, alike and yet different. Though public institutions attract their share of top students, even the best are limited by the mandate to serve the residents of their state. Though the quality of their academic programs may be just as strong, public

TIP

Among American colleges, age often equals prestige. The eight schools of the Ivy League were all founded before 1776.

universities can seldom match the atmosphere of intellectual stimulation at the best private institutions.

The case for private colleges and universities rests mainly on intangibles. Each family must make its own decision.

PERSONALITY

Colleges are just like people. They have personalities, too. Some are laid-back and some are intense; some are friendly and some are reserved; some are spirited and some are blasé; some are conservative and some are liberal. These personalities have extraordinary staying power. Benjamin Franklin founded the University of Pennsylvania in 1740 to further the "useful arts," and today Penn still reflects his career-oriented approach to education.

Often, high school students don't understand just how wide the differences in personality can be. There are some colleges that resemble 1960s communes; others where smoking, drinking, and even dancing are banned. You'll find football, fraternities, and homecoming weekends at some colleges; at others, the students scoff at the mere mention of such frivolities. At some colleges, homosexuality is a chic alternative lifestyle that many students try out because it is cool or "politically correct"; at many others, gays and lesbians are practically tarred and feathered if they come out of the closet.

To highlight some of the contrasts, we offer descriptions of two colleges that represent the poles of the spectrum. They're both the same size—approximately 1,200 students—and both have combined average SAT scores in the 1200 range. In short, they are both highly selective, small liberal arts colleges.

School #1 is University of the South, a Tennessee liberal arts college, with a handful of graduate students, known informally as Sewanee (because that's the name of the town). The first thing you'll notice on visiting Sewanee is that most of the men are wearing jackets and ties, while most of the women are wearing makeup and skirts. Forty years ago most colleges had a similar dress code; today Sewanee is one of a handful. The majority of students pledge fraternities and sororities, and social life revolves around a never-ending stream of "big-weekend" beer bashes. The biggest of them all is homecoming weekend, where the whole school gets a date and dresses up for a huge see-and-be-seen fashion show that includes innumerable cocktail parties before and after. Conservative, well-heeled, and All-American, Sewanee is the perfect place for a carefree 1950s-style college education. In the words of one student, Sewanee has "the happiest college student body I have ever encountered."

No one would ever say such a thing about Bard College, a school of similar size about an hour north of New York City. Though the students may find happiness there too, it is well hidden beneath a thick veneer of liberal artistic angst. Bard students, it seems, carry the weight of the world on their shoulders. If there is an oppressed group anywhere to be found, Bard students can be counted on to buy T-shirts, sell buttons, and organize protests on its behalf. As for clothes, you would be hard-pressed to find a Bard man who even owns a jacket and tie. Nor would the typical Bard woman be caught dead in a dress—unless it was paired with combat boots. Jewelry and makeup worn in traditional ways are nonexistent, but there is plenty of spiked hair, fluorescent hair, tattoos, and earrings protruding from every conceivable body part. As for football and fraternities? Take a wild guess. Bard students will march and protest at the drop of hat, but they never go to football games. Far-left politics and nonconformity are the rule at this free-spirited New York State school.

Admittedly, these two examples are near the extremes. But they illustrate some universal tendencies. Where would you feel more comfortable? Do you have a strong anti-establishment streak? Do you feel confined by the conventional norms of our society? Or are you looking for a more traditional college experience? Fortunately for most of us, the majority of American colleges lie somewhere between the Sewanees and Bards of the world. Most colleges include a mix of progressive elements and traditional ones. Once you've figured out the combination you're looking for, the hard part is finding the right mix in a college. How to do that is one of the topics that we deal with in the next chapter.

4
Getting a Jump Start

Y ou've got a mailbox full of brochures and a slew of unanswered questions. So many colleges out there. So much information to absorb. Fortunately, the college admissions process is not a sprint but a marathon. No one is going to demand that you pick a college today. Or next week. Every time you read a brochure, talk to a friend, or visit a college, you add a few more bits of information to your memory bank. The hard part is maintaining your resolve when the whole thing seems hopeless. Disaster comes only when you allow yourself to be paralyzed.

By now, you've thought a little about yourself and your priorities, and you've had a general introduction to some of the different types of schools. Below, we offer six ways to get a start on finding a list of colleges that meet your needs. Notice we said "get a start." The purpose of these methods is merely to identify possibilities, colleges that fit one or more of your criteria and may be worth further investigation. The real work, that of choosing from among those possibilities, comes later.

Of the six methods listed here, no one way is the best. We even recommend doing three or four of them simultaneously. Each one you try can provide another piece of the puzzle. Whatever your strategy, the most important thing is merely to get the ball rolling. Now is the time to start naming names—to develop a list of approximately twenty to thirty colleges that you would like to learn more about.

SIX WAYS TO JUMP-START YOUR COLLEGE SEARCH

1. **Read Chapter 6, "The One-Hour College Finder."** This chapter is designed for students applying to selective schools. It provides lists and thumbnail sketches of colleges appropriate for students with various academic and nonacademic interests. Use it as a seedbed for ideas on colleges to investigate further in the next phase.

2. **Browse a college guide.** Consult "Where to Learn More" (page 98) for some ideas on good guides. For ambitious students, we recommend—surprise!—*The Fiske Guide to Colleges,* which includes in-depth profiles of more than three hundred of the best colleges. This is the best place to draw a bead on the personalities of the schools. When you find one that seems like a good match, make a note and then look in the last line of the article for the "overlaps." These are the other colleges to which students most often apply when considering the one profiled in the article. Then read about those colleges, and consult their overlaps. Within a few weeks, you'll have the beginnings of a good list.

3. **Run a computer search.** If your typical day includes any time at all in front of a computer screen, you'll probably want to use your computer to look for colleges. Most high school guidance offices have college-search software. If not, you can buy your own or find one on the World Wide Web (see "Where to Learn More," page 98). In a nutshell, these programs allow you to make choices among ten to twenty variables (for example, size, location, majors). Once you have input your specifications in each category, the program identifies all the colleges that meet your criteria. Unfortunately, computer programs are generally not much help when it comes to the personality of the schools, but they can be a big help in sifting through more objective criteria. See also "High-Tech Sources," page 26.

4. **Poll friends, teachers, and relatives.** If you're a junior in high school, there is no better place to begin a college search than with members of the senior class whom you respect and who share your interests. Why not benefit from their extra year of experience? Older friends at colleges you are considering can also be a fertile source of information, as long as you keep in mind that the same student who sings his school's praises during spring break may curse it up and down if you happen to catch him during exams. If there are any

teachers you respect and who know you well, by all means ask if they have any schools to recommend. Try to keep an open mind to any and all suggestions at this early stage. As long as no one is trying to cram anything down your throat, welcome the free advice and take it seriously.

5. **Talk to some experts.** Few people are better positioned to give advice than those who work in a field that interests you, and this method is particularly useful for those who have a particular career path in mind. Think you might be interested in architecture? See if someone in your circle of friends and relatives knows an architect whom you might be able to call. An even bigger coup would be to talk to someone involved in hiring architects. Another approach is to visit a college, not necessarily to look at that particular school but as a fact-finding mission on a particular career. Most college admissions offices will happily help you arrange an appointment with professors in just about any field. See also "Private Counselors," page 28.

6. **Read college view books and catalogues.** This method comes last—mainly to follow up leads from other sources. That's because anything produced by the colleges—from posters to videos to World Wide Web sites—is little more than glitzy advertising. You probably wouldn't buy a 50-cent soft drink on the basis of an ad, so why buy a $100,000 college education based on one? In the next chapter, we discuss the right way to use college literature. For now we merely say: buyer beware.

Discerning readers will note that we have yet to mention one of the most important sources of college information: the guidance counselor. Ideally, your counselor will be your most trusted ally throughout the process. Unfortunately, most counselors are overworked, underpaid, and responsible for everything from suicide prevention to watering the principal's plants. If you don't have ready access to a good counselor, this book can act as a good substitute.

We save the counselor for last to encourage you to do a little homework *before* meeting with your counselor. Any of the six strategies above would be a great prelude to your first meeting with a guidance counselor during, say, January of your junior year. For starters, the counselor just might fall out of her chair at the sight of an applicant who has actually done some homework. In case you need reminding, the guidance counselor is probably the person who will fill out the secondary school evaluation form that goes to all your colleges. Many use the college search as an important measuring stick for applicants like you. The more organized and ahead of the game you are, the better the recommendation you are likely to get.

The second reason to do some initial spadework before the meeting is more immediate. The best use of the guidance counselor is as a sounding board and a reality check. At very small high schools, the counselor may be able to give you a personalized list of colleges, but most schools are way too big for that kind of service. Every counselor can respond to a list and provide some idea of whether or not you are being realistic in your plans. Many keep records of how past applicants from your school fared, and they may be able to give you an informed opinion of your chances for admission. They can also discuss the pros and cons of the colleges on your list, and perhaps suggest others where students with your interests and grades have had success. Finally, they can give you the names of everyone from your school who attends the colleges you're interested in.

As the application process moves forward, your counselor should continue to be a vital resource. Make a point of seeing him or her as much as possible without being a pest. In the words of Teresa Lahti from Kalamazoo College, "Start early in developing a relationship with your counselor by seeking advice on curriculum choices, activities, etc. before you begin to seek help in more pressured situations."

Though most counselors want only what is best for their counselees, watch out for the ones who have other agendas. Some counselors have pet schools that they peddle indiscriminately, while others are under pressure from principals or parents to steer applicants toward (or away from) certain "designer label" schools. Some like to place students at tried-and-true in-state schools while scoffing at the idea of attending one that may be "too far away." Still others will try to discourage you from applying to certain colleges because they think too many other students from your school are already applying there. Richard Hallin of Eckerd College warns, "Beware of the guidance counselors who attempt to restrict options by giving such advice as: it's too costly or too far away; no one I know goes there; it's not right for you. A good guidance counselor will expand horizons and help find information." In any case, do not hesitate to ask your counselor to explain and justify his or her recommendations.

Remember also that even the best counselors aren't infallible. All know more about some schools (especially those nearby) than others, and occasionally their preconceptions will be dated or based on inaccurate information. Whenever possible, double-check what your counselor says with teachers, college guides, and other sources.

As white-knuckle time nears, give the counselor plenty of lead time before deadlines. Don't just assume that everything is done once you hand in your part of the application. You will probably have five applications to

> **TIP**

> Be wary of sources that purport to offer numerical rank-ings of the colleges. Such efforts give an illusion of precision while missing the main point of the college search: different schools are right for different people. Avoid at all costs **The Gourman Report**, a book that uses bogus methodology to generate bizarre rankings. The annual **U.S. News & World Report** rankings can be useful as a seedbed of possible choices, as long as you realize that the difference between #5 and #15 is probably insignificant. Their rankings change yearly with little rhyme or reason—the better to sell each new edition of the magazine.

process; your counselor may have five hundred. A little double checking on your part is a wise move. Even the best guidance offices slip up occasion-ally. Polite but diligent follow-up with your guidance counselor and the colleges can help prevent a snafu that could jeopardize your chances.

HIGH-TECH SOURCES

One of the fastest-growing places to learn about colleges is your computer screen via disk, CD-ROM, or an online service. With a few keystrokes, applicants can get information that once required a letter or a trip to the library. Though books are still the best place to get in-depth evaluative information about colleges and the college search, the computer has now taken its place alongside them as an important tool. Some of the best uses of the computer in college admissions include: (1) searching out colleges and scholarships using an objective database, (2) communicating with colleges and filing applications, and (3) registering for standardized tests and order-ing products online.

One commonly used electronic tool in the college search is CD-ROM software, available in computer stores and most guidance offices. Students can use it to search for colleges and scholarships, and with Internet access, to request information directly from the schools. Many of these programs also incorporate an interactive element, allowing students to view film clips describing the colleges and take "virtual" tours. Despite the engaging inter-face, the value of these programs is limited once the student has generated a list of schools. For financial reasons, most of the software companies are in cahoots with the colleges, meaning that the descriptions are largely public-relations snow jobs. The computer is fine for making a list of, say, all the schools in North Carolina with an enrollment of 2,000 students or fewer. But if you want any information on *how good* those colleges are, you'll still need to consult a print college guide. Some of the most prominent college books are now available in a CD-ROM version, though at a higher price than the book edition. Your best move is to check out the guidance office to see what disk and CD-ROM sources are available there. For your own purchases, books are still probably the best bet. Though CD-ROM is still relatively new, it may soon be rendered obsolete by the Internet. Most CD-ROM companies offer similar services online; some companies charge a fee and some do not.

The world of cyberspace offers an unlimited source of college information. A good place to start is the World Wide Web, where virtually all colleges have a home page. Some are still just billboards with basic information; others include dozens of additional screens produced by various departments and student organizations within the institution. Much of their content is a rehash of printed materials, but persistent surfers will uncover layers of detail about particular departments and professors that is unavailable anywhere else. In addition, these sites are an excellent source of e-mail addresses for admissions officers, professors, and other university personnel. A growing number of college Web sites also include applications that can be downloaded, completed, and filed electronically. By cyberspace standards, downloading an application is still maddeningly slow, but the process gets easier with each passing year.

Applying via computer is definitely the wave of the future—but more on that when the time comes to talk about filing your applications.

Other major players in the college search have also taken advantage of the Internet. Makers of standardized tests have come online with a full range of services available via the Web, including test registration and orders for publications. Other outfits have set up sites intended for college applicants that include some or all of the following: college-search programs, scholarship services, test prep, question-and-answer bulletin boards, and electronic stores that allow you to order print sources online. The main problem with all this information is quality control. Though the Internet may be glitzy, the quality of the data backing it up is often shaky. A lot of companies who know more about computers than they do about colleges are trying to cash in on a trendy new medium. Be stingy with your credit card number and don't even think about putting money down until you have surfed a number of sites. One rule of thumb for using the Internet: Look for companies whose names you know from print sources. They're the ones with a proven track record. (See Chapter 7, "Where to Learn More.")

If you feel as if the cyber revolution has left you in the dust, don't panic. Applicants can still do just fine with books, paper, and pen. The computer merely offers a parallel means to the same end. High schools are notoriously slow in assimilating new technology, and full Internet access is still years away for many. Even if your guidance office doesn't have the latest software, it can still give you good advice about colleges along with the print sources described in "Where to Learn More" (page 98).

PRIVATE COUNSELORS

Technology aside, some school guidance offices are simply incapable of offering good advice on college. Many public school districts have experienced deep budget cuts in recent years, resulting in staggering workloads for overburdened counselors. If you are one of those unfortunate applicants who cannot get adequate advice from your school, you may want to consider hiring a private college counselor. It'll cost you a fair piece of change— from a few hundred dollars up to $2,000 for a full admissions-process package—but the bill could be worth it if the counselor you hire is a good one. Services range from helping you draw up an application list to advice on test taking, filling out applications, writing essays, and managing the wait list. An experienced independent counselor can be invaluable as a sounding board and as a source of knowledge about the colleges. Just don't sign on under the illusion that he or she will somehow get you in through inside connections or "pulling strings." Used this way, independent counselors are little more than hired lobbyists, a fact not lost on the admissions officers. As a rule, it is best to make sure that your independent counselor's "fingerprints" don't show up on your applications and raise questions as to whether the work is really yours. If you can't stand on your own qualifications, no amount of high-priced consulting and packaging will make any difference.

A final word of advice as you seek college information: Listen to your parents. Improbable as it may seem, good ol' Mom and Dad can often be an excellent source of information. Even when they seem hopelessly out of touch with your world, you might be surprised by how much they really know about you and what makes you happy. Furthermore, your parents will never forget (and you shouldn't either) that *they* are the ones who are going to pay the bills. Try to settle on some ground rules from the beginning as to how much they are willing to pay, how much input they will have in the final choice, and so on. In general, it is best to avoid the extremes—relying exclusively on their advice or locking them out of the process altogether. Your parents should recognize that the choice of college (within limits) is yours to make, while at the same time you can acknowledge that they have an important role to play. A firm understanding early in the process can prevent a lot of heartache and bitterness at the end.

By the spring of your junior year, your college search should be in high gear. You should be able to winnow your list of twenty to thirty "possibles" down to a more manageable list of ten or twelve by about May or June. That's when the serious comparison shopping really begins.

5
Cutting Through the Propaganda

I f you're wondering why Joe Admissions Officer from Most Desirable University—which you've never heard of—sent you a warm, personal letter and a slick multicolored brochure that reads "Uncle Joe Wants YOU to go to Most Desirable U.," chalk it up to what one admissions dean calls "the mass-marketing mania." The truth is, Uncle Joe wants you—and the 100,000 or so other prospective applicants who also received his letter.

When the pool of college-age students began shrinking in the early 1980s, recruitment programs kicked into high gear. The competition for students has since become increasingly cutthroat, and even elite institutions are hawking their wares with a vengeance. When "sell, sell, sell" is the motto, truth in advertising often takes a beating. We're not accusing the colleges of lying, exactly, but some of them come pretty close. Don't play the role of starry-eyed sucker. Kick the tires, look under the hood, and find out exactly what you'll get for all that money.

College literature is a good place to cut your teeth as a comparison shopper. It can be fun. You'll soon be able to pick out all the hidden ploys and not-so-subtle persuasions built into the view books, brochures, and catalogues that will be bombarding your mailbox. You can also find some valuable information for your college search, but only if you read with a critical eye.

WHERE IT COMES FROM

How did *your* mailbox get chosen as the pipeline for all this advertising? Think back to the last time you took the PSAT, SAT I or II, or ACT. In addition to answering some questions about yourself, those forms asked if you wanted to receive a free service—the Student Search Service for the PSAT and SAT or the Educational Opportunity Service for the ACT.

The SAT box looks like this:

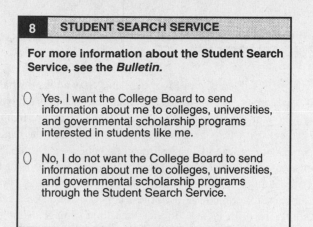

| 8 | STUDENT SEARCH SERVICE |

For more information about the Student Search Service, see the *Bulletin*.

○ Yes, I want the College Board to send information about me to colleges, universities, and governmental scholarship programs interested in students like me.

○ No, I do not want the College Board to send information about me to colleges, universities, and governmental scholarship programs through the Student Search Service.

Item 8 on the SAT I registration form from the 1995–96 Admissions Testing Program Registration Form and Student Descriptive Questionnaire, copyright 1995 by College Entrance Examination Board and Educational Testing Service

If you checked yes, you authorized the administrator of that test to sell your name, address, test scores, and the personal information you provided to any college admissions office that wants to buy it. Colleges purchase lists of the students who fall into specific "target" categories broken down by:

test scores
family income
fancy zip codes
intended major
ethnic or religious background
high school grade point average

The list includes almost everything except sexual preference. The College Board's Student Search Service sells millions of names every year to more than 1,200 colleges and educational organizations. When you factor in those fees, plus the cost of printing and mailing the brochures, colleges invest a pretty penny to court you through the U.S. Postal Service. Receiving promotional literature is not an invitatic.. to attend, but colleges wouldn't waste the money on students who are unrealistic candidates. With a pair of 350s on the SAT I, you won't be hearing from Yale.

PICKING THROUGH IT

Most of your mail will consist of brochures and view books—what the colleges call "search pieces." These are the college admissions equivalent of a thirty-second commercial. Just as a soft-drink maker or tire manufacturer does, the college often pays a marketing firm to help hone the message. On TV, the persuaders use catchy jingles, gurgling babies, celebrities. In higher education, the marketers generally try to sell an image. Among the most popular is the aura of traditional college life: white columns, ivy-covered walls, and majestic trees aflame with the colors of autumn on a crisp afternoon. Another favorite is the "hipper-than-thou" image, which usually includes splashy New Age script, loud colors, and pictures pasted at odd angles.

If you want to play a game, try guessing which photos are staged and which are candid. (Hint: Any picture of three or more people in which all are facing the camera is probably staged.)

Perhaps we are too cynical. Though view books usually say more about the skills of the marketing firms than the quality of the colleges, there are a few things you can learn. Pay attention to the message amid the puffery. What are the two or three basic ideas being conveyed? What does the college want you to know about it? Look for a business reply card or an order form in the back. Or give the admissions office a call or an e-mail message telling them you want more information. But beware: any show of interest triggers lots more mail from the computer that controls the whole process.

Lest there be any doubt, view books are probably the least useful kind of college literature. More helpful is the college's catalogue, an official document that lists course offerings, faculty, rules and regulations, the calendar, and so on. Since a catalogue doesn't try to sell you anything, it is a welcome refuge for reliable information. But because catalogues are big and expensive to print and mail, colleges usually reserve them for serious customers who request them. As an alternative to the postman, growing numbers of colleges make them available via the World Wide Web.

Look at how the catalogue is divided and how much space is allocated to various departments or majors. This gives you an idea of the college's academic layout. For example, is there a separate division of environmental studies, or are those students lumped in with the biology majors? Read the short bios of the faculty members. Do they all have their Ph.D.s? Did they earn them at creditable institutions? Does each department have a good mix of faculty who specialize in different areas of your intended major? Find the section that discusses freshman requirements and when students must declare their majors. Skim through the history of the college. How long has it been around? Who founded it and why?

A PEEK BEHIND THE STATISTICS

Another piece of literature that you should definitely consult is the college's report on its admissions statistics and student body. Most colleges refer to this document as their "Profile"; others call it "Report to Secondary Schools" or "Admissions Report." This is the place where you'll find the statistics on a college's acceptance rate, SAT profile, geographical distribution, and a host of other important topics. You'll also find the potential for deception. Since colleges live and die by how selective the public thinks they are, the temptation to fudge the numbers often proves too much. "I have learned over the years not to trust the data that admissions people give to the public," says one financial-aid official who chose to remain nameless, "They gild every lily in sight."

Of the various statistics, applicants inevitably zero in on SAT I profiles first. The most common mistake is to view "median" or "average" freshman SAT scores as cutoffs. If a college says that last year's freshmen had median SAT scores of 600 on the verbal section and you got a 570, the temptation is to think that you don't have a shot at that institution.

Think again. Median scores tell you where the middle of the class fell. In the instance above, half of the class had scores above 600, while half scored below that figure. For a more accurate picture of where you stand, find out the college's SAT ranges that encompass the middle half of the class—from the 25th to the 75th percentile. In general, this figure will range 40 to 50 points on either side of the median score. For example, if the median is 600, then the middle half of the freshman class will probably have scores between 550 and 650. Furthermore, many colleges exclude certain "special admits" from their reports. With one eye on the selectivity rankings, they lop off the scores of foreign students, the economically disadvantaged, children of alumni, minorities, and other groups. The result is an artificially inflated profile. This widespread practice became a national scandal after a *Wall Street Journal* exposé a few years ago. Another widely used deception is to report the SAT ranges of *admitted* applicants rather than *enrolled* applicants. The admitted range is always higher because top students will always have more options to enroll elsewhere. The good news for you is that the real SAT profile is often lower than what the colleges advertise to the public.

If your scores fall within the range of the middle half, you can assume that you will be comfortable academically at that institution. If your scores would put you in the upper quartile, you might want to consider a more academically demanding institution. If your scores would put you in the bottom quartile, you probably want to think about whether that school would be too much of a struggle.

The listing of the high school class rank also provides fertile ground for creative marketing. Most schools quote the number of their students who ranked in the top tenth, the second tenth, and so on for their most recent freshman class. In fine print at the bottom is a category for "no rank," which generally includes about a third of the students. The secret here is that the unranked group generally comes from high-powered private schools. Even students with mediocre grades from these schools are welcomed by many colleges, and the absence of a rank gives the colleges cover to accept less-than-stellar performers without fessing up publicly. If you attend a private or parochial school, don't be intimidated by a sky-high class-rank listing.

Despite all the tinkering around the edges, a college's profile can still

TIP To help assess your chances at a particular college, talk to your guidance counselor. Most will have records of how past applicants from your school with similar scores and grade point averages have fared.

give you an excellent idea of your chances for admission. Assume that it is somewhat inflated but still reasonably accurate.

The SAT and class-rank statistics are most meaningful if examined in combination with the school's acceptance rate. If that rate is 30 percent or below, you probably need credentials that compare favorably with the SAT and class-rank listings to be a really strong candidate, unless you fall into a special admit category, such as a recruited athlete or an underrepresented minority. A college that accepts only 30 percent of applicants includes in those it rejects a high percentage of applicants with scores and grades that meet its profile. On the other hand, colleges accepting 60 or 70 percent will often admit candidates ranking well below the averages in the profile.

A second figure to which you should pay close attention is a college's "yield"—the percentage of accepted applicants who choose to enroll. The yield is harder to manipulate than the acceptance rate and is a good index of a college's desirability among applicants. Any college with a yield of 50 percent or higher is usually a first-choice school. A yield between 30 and 50 percent is average for a selective private college, while a figure lower than 30 indicates a college that is frequently used as a "safety school."

MORE FUDGE FROM THE CONFECTIONERY

Of all the statistics quoted by admissions offices, the most misused and misrepresented is the "student-faculty ratio." If a college claims to have a ratio of 12 to 1, don't think for a minute that your classes will only have twelve students in them. "Faculty" may include everyone from part-time lab assistants to medical and law professors who do not teach undergraduates. Moreover, even full-time faculty only teach two or three classes, whereas students take four or five. Large universities are especially brazen in over-

---

Cooking the Numbers

One of the dirty little secrets of college admissions is that selectivity can be easily manipulated. Several years ago a well-known women's college in New England was horrified to discover that it was taking four out of five applicants. So the next year it sent out a huge number of brochures and generated a lot more applications. Image problem solved.

---

stating the ratio, as they routinely include graduate students in the calculations. Small liberal arts colleges that don't have graduate programs are usually the most trustworthy on the student-faculty ratio. A better question is "What's the average size of classes taken by freshmen?" (see Chapter 14, "Surviving the Interview").

Another shady area is the percentage of graduates accepted at professional schools. Most colleges quote figures that are suspiciously high. One reason is that many schools pre-screen applicants to law and medical schools, recommending only the top ones for admission (and then counting in its percentage only those recommended). The percentage of students on financial aid is also a less-than-meaningful number that is tossed around in many profiles. "Financial aid" can include everything from a $20,000 grant to a loan at the market interest rate (see Chapter 18, "The New Financial-Aid Game").

We hope this tour through the jungle of college literature hasn't been too disconcerting. To be fair, the admissions people are less to blame than the university presidents, who have been known to fire admissions deans if the acceptance rate goes up or the SAT profile goes down. With so much uncertainty surrounding statistics, we conclude with the advice of Michael Behnke of MIT: "Figure out what question you're trying to get answered by looking at the statistics. Then ask the question and forget the statistics."

6
The One-Hour College Finder

B y now, you've done the equivalent of sticking your big toe in the water. You can stand there for hours, timidly gazing out over the ripples. Or you can breathe deeply and take the plunge. In this chapter, we offer one way to generate a reasonable list of colleges in an hour or two even if you're starting from scratch.

Consider this your pocket map to the higher-education universe. We've divided several hundred of the most prominent schools into categories based on a variety of factors that will be significant in your college search. Where appropriate, we have included the sort of thumbnail assessment that you might get from a good college counselor. Read the whole chapter if you like, or simply browse the lists that seem most interesting. As you go, make a note of the colleges that seem right for you. If you already have particular schools in mind, refer to the index at the back of the book for the pages where they are featured. We suggest that you use this section as a shorthand directory to *The Fiske Guide to Colleges*. The majority of the schools mentioned in this book are described there in much greater detail.

Please note that these lists represent subjective judgments. Though based on years of observing higher education (and extensive consulting with other experts), the opinions expressed here are just that—opinions. We recommend that you use the lists to help broaden your horizons, and beware of eliminating colleges from consideration merely because they don't show up in one of our categories.

"The One-Hour College Finder" is divided into two sections. The first, beginning below, is intended primarily for students intending to major in the liberal arts and the sciences. Beginning on page 81, we offer lists of colleges strong in selected pre-professional fields. Some of these schools also offer liberal arts degrees; others focus exclusively on pre-professional training.

THE ELITE

These are the places that ooze prestige from every crack and crevice of their ivy-covered walls. If you want to scale these lofty heights, you'd better come armed with an impeccable transcript, stratospheric scores, and/or championship-level talent in one or more extracurricular areas. The main dilemma: Do you prefer a liberal arts college offering small classes, close interaction with faculty, and a better chance to be involved in the extracurricular life of the community? Or do you want a comprehensive university with world-class facilities and a world-class name? As we noted in Chapter 3, "The College Universe," many educators favor the former. That's one reason why a high percentage of the children of college professors enroll at the elite small colleges, and why graduates of such schools have always earned Ph.D.s in large numbers. The prestigious universities have historically been feeders of the business and professional worlds rather than the academic world. (The University of Chicago is a conspicuous exception.)

No matter what your aspirations, you'll find outstanding opportunities at both types of institutions.

The Elite Private Universities

Brown University. A charter member of the hot college club . . . Flooded with applicants seeking Ivy education without all the stress . . . Has toughened requirements but still fighting "soft" image . . . Bashed by conservatives as hotbed of political correctness.

University of Chicago. Less selective than any other university on this list, and far better than two-thirds of them . . . Only true scholars apply, hence the acceptance rate is higher . . . Known as "the teacher of teachers" . . . Mothers tremble at the thought of the South Side of Chicago, but Hyde Park is among the nation's most interesting neighborhoods.

Columbia University. Three things set Columbia apart from the other great universities: Manhattan, Manhattan, and Manhattan . . . Renowned core curriculum gives substance and coherence to freshman and sophomore years . . . Harlem is only a few blocks away, but safety is no more a concern here than on any other urban campus.

Cornell University. Reputation as a pressure cooker comes from pre-professional attitude and "we try harder" mentality . . . Offers more diversity than other Ivy institutions because of its public colleges . . . The

Greek system plays a key role in social life . . . Beautiful Finger Lakes are a haven for winter sports.

Dartmouth College. The smallest Ivy and the one with the strongest emphasis on undergraduates . . . Still the most traditional student body in the Ivy League, but not the hotbed of extreme conservatism that some believe it to be . . . Administration has worked hard to shed "animal house" image by bringing in more scholars . . . If you love the outdoors, you'll be in heaven.

Duke University. The rising star of the South, now competes on even footing with the Ivies and Stanford . . . Offers unusual combination of big-time sports and big-time academics . . . Though student body is national, Southern location and Greek life give Duke a more traditional college feel than most Northern schools . . . Not as intellectual as the Ivies, but more fun.

Georgetown University. The most selective of the nation's Roman Catholic–affiliated schools . . . Washington, D.C., location draws students of all faiths in droves . . . Unparalleled access to the corridors of power attracts politicos of all types, and undergraduate business program is also tops . . . A more conservative institution than most of its elite counterparts.

Harvard University. The end of the rainbow for thousands of the world's best and brightest . . . Student body is the most high-powered in the nation, and opportunities are unparalleled . . . But are classes too big? And how accessible are professors? . . . Irresistible lure of the Harvard name and Boston/Cambridge area mean only a handful turn down acceptance from the Big H.

Massachusetts Institute of Technology. Tops in technology but also strong in the social sciences . . . Admission is ultracompetitive in the natural sciences and engineering, less so in other areas . . . Men outnumber women two to one, but Boston-area location ensures a steady stream of new faces . . . "Sink or swim" climate not for the faint of heart.

University of Pennsylvania. Prototypical urban university with an emphasis on practical education that dates back to founder Ben Franklin . . . The most pre-professional of the Ivy schools, including the only elite undergraduate business school . . . School spirit and Greek life make Penn more fun than other Ivies . . . Still confused with Penn State after 250 years.

Princeton University. Has risen a notch or two in recent years because of safety woes at Yale and Harvard . . . Increasingly, the favored alternative to Harvard in the East . . . Traditionally popular with Southerners and still conservative-leaning . . . A close second to Dartmouth as the most undergraduate-friendly of the major universities.

Stanford University. On a par with Harvard in resources and prestige . . . Free of the gloom that seems to hang over high-powered Eastern campuses, but how serious is the intellectual atmosphere? . . . Beautiful weather most of the year is so-o-o-o-o tempting . . . Easterners who visit in February may never be seen or heard from again.

Yale University. Hurt badly in the nineties by urban violence in gritty New Haven . . . *Vanity Fair* proclaims "The Death of Yale," but the reports are greatly exaggerated . . . Yale is still a mecca in the humanities and social sciences, and has the best arts programs in the Ivies . . . Widely imitated residential colleges help Yale deliver the best of large and small.

The Elite Liberal Arts Colleges

Amherst College. Long viewed as the most elite of the "Little Ivies" . . . Known for well-rounded "gentleperson jocks" . . . Near-perfect location combines rural beauty with cultured western Massachusetts . . . Ties to Hampshire, Mount Holyoke, UMass/Amherst, and Smith via Five-College Consortium gives Amherst the best of large and small.

Bowdoin College. Quietly prestigious Maine school that specializes in Yankee individualism . . . No SAT I required for admission . . . Strong science programs, and outdoor enthusiasts benefit from proximity to the Atlantic coast and upstate wilderness . . . Succulent dining hall food will give Mom a run for her money.

Bryn Mawr College. The most intellectual of the women's colleges . . . Politics range from liberal to radical . . . Do Bryn Mawrters take themselves a bit too seriously? . . . Still benefits from proximity to Haverford, but the latter's decision to go coed in the early eighties damaged that relationship.

Carleton College. Less selective than Amherst and Williams largely because of central Minnesota location . . . Our choice as the best liberal arts college in the Midwest . . . Predominantly liberal school, but not to the extremes of its more anti-establishment cousins . . . Tunnels between buildings help Carls beat the winter blues.

Davidson College. Gets the nod as best liberal arts college in the South . . . Liberal by Southern standards, conservative by Northern ones . . . Small-town location near bustling Charlotte . . . Curriculum includes extensive core requirements . . . Social life dominated by fraternity-like eating clubs.

Haverford College. Secluded Quaker enclave in Philadelphia's affluent Main Line suburbs . . . Superb blend of traditional and progressive . . . Old-fashioned honor code governs all facets of life . . . With only 1,000 students, the most intimate of the colleges on this list. An underrated gem.

Pomona College. Hands down, the finest liberal arts college in the West . . . Serious intellectual climate combines with close proximity to an interesting mix of outstanding colleges in the Claremont group . . . Location an hour east of Los Angeles would be ideal except for choking smog that hangs over the area much of the year.

Swarthmore College. Pound for pound, the most intellectual school in the nation . . . Combines social activism with perverse pride in failures of athletic teams . . . Closeness of student-faculty relations among the best in the nation . . . Likely to overwhelm all but the most committed scholars.

Wellesley College. Most successful of the former Seven Sisters in preserving admissions selectivity . . . Location in suburban Boston offers ties to Harvard, MIT, and the many other area schools . . . Campus is a strong candidate for the most beautiful in the nation . . . Nice balance of liberal and conservative helps fend off political correctness.

Wesleyan University. Known as the most individualistic and liberal of the Little Ivies . . . Ranks with Oberlin as the coed college with the longest tradition of outreach to minorities . . . National in scope but draws more streetwise Easterners than some of its competitors . . . Campus is nice, but Middletown suffers from post-industrial depression.

Williams College. A crème de la crème liberal arts college that occupies a campus of surpassing beauty in the foothills of the Berkshires . . . Has shaken preppy image but still attracts its share of intelligent, well-toned jocks . . . Williamstown is isolated for some and absolute paradise for others.

RISING STARS

Though we call these "Rising Stars," there is nothing new about the superb academic quality and exclusive admissions standards at any of these schools. As a group, they are relative newcomers to the super-elite of American higher education. Most have benefited from recent surges in applications, and a number are actually more selective than some of the colleges on the elite list. They tend to be in "hot" locations and are well positioned to continue on an upward trajectory.

Bates College. Bastion of egalitarianism in southern Maine . . . One of the first coed schools in the nation, never had frats . . . Among the handful of colleges in the nation that doesn't require standardized tests . . . Unusual sense of camaraderie that includes everyone from the president to the maintenance staff . . . Blighted Lewiston is the only downer.

Colby College. More and more students are discovering this Northeasterly outpost of higher education . . . Picturesque small-town setting is a short hop from the seacoast or the Maine wilderness . . . No frats since the college abolished them in 1984 . . . Reputation as a happy, healthy place.

Emory University. Has finally hit the big time with strategic Atlanta location and massive gifts from Coke founder . . . Home to large numbers of transplanted Yankees and Midwesterners . . . Crowded suburban campus lacks elite ambience . . . Well positioned to give Duke a run for its money as the leading university in the Southeast.

Middlebury College. Vermont liberal arts college moving up rapidly on the prestige-o-meter . . . Beautiful Green Mountain location combines with strong programs in hot areas like international studies and environmental science . . . Known worldwide for its summer foreign-language programs . . . Students can substitute SAT II subject tests for SAT I.

Northwestern University. Immensely popular university by the shores of Lake Michigan north of Chicago . . . Attracts droves of preprofessionals in areas like business, journalism, engineering, and pre-med . . . Combines high-powered academics with Big Ten athletics . . . Another Rose Bowl for the Wildcats?

Rice University. Is there any college in the nation hotter than Rice? . . . Offers science and engineering programs on a par with the nation's best at a fraction of the cost . . . Huge endowment helps Rice offer bargain-basement tuition . . . Out-of-staters should make sure they like the Texas atmosphere before diving in.

Tufts University. Prestigious medium-size university in a working-class Boston suburb . . . A recent spate of construction offers testimony that Tufts is on the move . . . Best known for international relations and engineering, though offerings are strong across the board . . . A quick subway ride away from everything "The Hub" has to offer.

Vanderbilt University. A more "Southern" place than competitors Duke, Emory, and Tulane . . . Traditional favorite of affluent Atlanta and Birmingham suburbs . . . Secluded Nashville campus among the prettiest in the South . . . Becoming more national, and the admissions office lures increasing numbers of non-Southerners.

Wake Forest University. Another middle-size (5,500) Southern university on the move . . . Conservative by national standards, though severed ties to ultraconservative Southern Baptists in 1986 . . . ACC athletics and Greek parties shape social scene . . . Strategic central North Carolina location accessible to mountains, beaches, and famous research triangle.

☞**See Also**

> **Bard College** (Top Nonconformist Colleges)
> **Duke University** (The Elite Private Universities)
> **Grove City College** (Top Conservative Colleges)
> **Spelman College** (Historically Black Colleges and Universities)
> **University of Virginia** (The Budget Ivy League)

TOP COLLEGES, BETTER ODDS

These are for students who plunge into major depression every time they look at Ivy League acceptance rates. Instead of beating your head endlessly against that ivy-covered brick wall, why not consider one of the outstanding schools on this list? You'll get an education on a par with the fanciest designer-label college, maybe better, and all these places have excellent national reputations. The only difference is that applicants are not clamoring for admission in quite the same numbers.

The reasons vary. Some have such strong reputations for academic rigor that mediocre students would never dare apply. As they say in admissions, the applicant pool is "self-selected." Whereas the Ivies always attract stacks of applications from wannabes, hangers-on, and various other prestige hounds, the ratio of serious students tends to be higher at many of these schools (which is, by the way, a good reason why the acceptance rate is not always the best indicator of a school's quality).

In other cases, location plays a role. Many Easterners seem to think they'll fall off the edge of the earth if they venture past Buffalo or Pittsburgh, but it just so happens that many of the finest colleges in the nation are tucked away in places like Ohio, Iowa, and Minnesota. The schools in trendy locales like Boston or Washington, D.C., tend be deluged with applications, while better ones in the Midwest often attract far fewer. The South can also be fertile hunting ground, especially for students who like the conservative flavor of that region.

All of the colleges on this list are well known in higher-education circles, especially in the admissions offices of top graduate and professional programs.

Case Western Reserve University. Middle-size Ohio university known for science and engineering . . . Best kept secret: the arts are just as good . . . Long name is the result of an unlikely marriage between a technical institute and a liberal arts college . . . Located in a so-so neighborhood but adjacent to Cleveland's cultural and artistic hub.

Grinnell College. Is this Heaven? No, it's Grinnell College, tucked away in the Iowa cornfields . . . Competes with the top liberal arts colleges in the nation, though hamstrung by location . . . Very liberal, attracts lots of Chicagoans . . . Savvy financial management has created huge endowment . . . With nation's highest literacy rate, Iowa gets a bad rap.

The Johns Hopkins University. The Hop makes this list mainly because of its (somewhat misleading) reputation as a pre-med factory . . . While future doctors stampede the admissions gate, humanists and social scientists can waltz in with much less difficulty . . . The heavyweight champ of federal grants . . . Located in downtown Baltimore.

Kenyon College. The quintessential small liberal arts college . . . Rural Ohio location is peaceful to some, isolated to others . . . Known for its humanities programs, especially English . . . Enrollment of 1,500 puts Kenyon on the small side of small . . . Unique sense of community between faculty and students.

Macalester College. Anyone considering liberal arts colleges *must* take a look . . . Charming suburban location in Minneapolis–St. Paul, one of the nation's most livable cities . . . More diversity and international flavor than many other more prestigious colleges . . . Huge endowment ranks high among elite private colleges.

Oberlin College. Combines a sterling reputation with moderate selectivity . . . First American college to open its doors to women and minorities . . . Long a haven for nonconformists, now trying to lure a few more middle-of-the-roaders . . . Top-notch conservatory and art gallery attract artists in droves.

Reed College. Legendary as a countercultural mecca and also for intense introspection . . . Required senior thesis would earn a master's degree at many schools . . . Low graduation rate attests that the Reed experience is overwhelming for some . . . Student body consists mainly of urbanites from both coasts.

University of Rochester. Nondescript name camouflages a distinguished private university . . . Close ties to Eastman School of Music are a boon for musicians . . . Other strengths include top science programs and innovative thematic freshman-year courses . . . Currently downsizing to recover from financial difficulties and boost selectivity.

Washington University (Missouri). Best private university between Chicago and San Francisco . . . Known primarily for professional programs such as business, engineering, and pre-med . . . Also superb in art . . . Inviting St. Louis campus in quiet suburban enclave . . . Increasing in selectivity but still often a second choice to Northwestern.

THE BEST BARGAINS

Anyone who purports to name the best college bargains begins on shaky ground. Every student has different needs and interests. What looks like a bargain to one person may be too expensive at any price for the next. For that reason, we offer several lists to cover our picks for the best bargains in American higher education. The Public Ivy League includes colleges and universities that enroll more than 5,000 students, while Small-College Bargains includes those that enroll under 5,000. We also offer a short section on public-university honors programs.

A quick caveat before you begin. Many of the colleges on the list are public universities, which have typically cost about a third to a half as much as their private counterparts. That has begun to change in recent years, however, as public university tuitions have begun to rise faster than those at private ones. As a general rule, out-of-staters can now expect to fork over about two-thirds of the price of a comparable private-school tuition—not quite the bargain rate of a few years ago but still a substantial savings.

The Budget Ivy League

This list includes most of the premier public universities in the nation. (A few of the most expensive ones, such as University of Michigan and University of Vermont, are listed under Other Well-Known Universities.) All combine superb academic programs and low cost. In-state tuition at each is approximately $5,000 or less. Out-of-state tuition ranges from $5,000 to $10,000, with three exceptions: University of Colorado/Boulder, University of Virginia, and College of William and Mary. Though these cost more than $10,000, they still qualify for "budget" status for their outstanding programs.

University of California/Berkeley. Makes this list because it is so cheap and so prestigious . . . Hurt badly in recent years by budget cuts and overcrowding . . . Self-starters will find unparalleled opportunities . . . More passive types will get lost in the herd.

University of California/Los Angeles. Ditto what we said about Berkeley . . . Cloistered away in exclusive Beverly Hills, UCLA is the more conservative of the two . . . The beach, the mountains, and chic Hollywood hangouts are all in easy reach . . . One of the world's best places to study the arts, film, or television.

University of Colorado/Boulder.   Offers the ultimate collegiate setting: a small, cultured city at the foot of the Rockies . . . Strongest in business, engineering, and the sciences . . . Out-of-staters account for a third of the students . . . Paradise for outdoor enthusiasts.

University of Florida.   One of the Southeast's premier universities . . . Highly touted honors program challenges the best students . . . Best known for its College of Journalism and Communications . . . Beware of huge classes and a housing crunch . . . Frats and football pace social life.

Georgia Institute of Technology.   The nation's top public technical institute . . . Ma Tech is a leader in every imaginable engineering field . . . Undergrads often suffer from large classes and the research orientation of the faculty . . . Atlanta and big-time sports teams offer plenty of excitement.

Indiana University.   The pride of the Hoosier state, now growing in national stature . . . A few strengths include business, journalism, international studies, and foreign languages . . . All students begin in the "university division" to ensure exposure to the liberal arts.

Miami University (Ohio).   Ohio's version of a public honors university . . . Beautiful campus evokes private-university atmosphere . . . Well-known business school sets the tone of campus . . . Known as the "mother of fraternities" because several began here . . . A bastion of Midwestern conservatism.

University of Minnesota/Twin Cities.   Northern goliath that is downsizing to provide better service to undergrads . . . Strong in the standard pre-professional areas plus forestry and Scandinavian studies . . . Housing shortage limits campus cohesiveness . . . The Twin Cities are among the nation's most livable.

College of New Jersey.   Formerly Trenton State University, this is a perennial in the "best buys" category . . . A former teachers' college that has remade itself into a selective university stressing the liberal arts, business, and accounting . . . Beautiful suburban campus with the "feel" of a private school.

State University of New York/Binghamton.   The best public university in the Northeast . . . Not as well known as UVA or Michigan because it has no big-time sports . . . Superb in the liberal arts as well as pre-professional areas . . . Weathering New York State budget cuts the sensible way: by downsizing and becoming more selective.

State University of New York/Geneseo. Smallish university (5,600) with strong programs in business and the liberal arts . . . Began as a teacher's college, and its female-to-male ratio is still two to one . . . Much excitement revolves around men's hockey team.

University of North Carolina/Chapel Hill. Close on the heels of UVA as the South's most prestigious state university . . . Honors program rates among the best in the nation . . . Unless you're a 300-pound noseguard or the next Michael Jordan, admission from out of state will be an uphill climb.

Rutgers University. The state university of New Jersey . . . Includes almost 50,000 students on six campuses . . . Rutgers College is the most selective, followed by Douglass (all women) and Livingston . . . Ninety percent of the students are homegrown Garden Staters.

University of Texas/Austin. Though the price tag is going up, UT is still the cheapest major university in the nation . . . The UT challenge: to avoid getting lost in the sea of 50,000 faces . . . Top programs include business, engineering, and Latin American studies . . . Liberal arts majors should check out the honors program.

Truman State University. Formerly Northeast Missouri State, Truman is rapidly becoming one of the heartland's finest colleges . . . After liberal arts core, many students opt for pre-professional programs . . . Small-town Missouri location.

University of Virginia. Competitiveness for out-of-state admission now at the Ivy League level . . . Mr. Jefferson's university remains one of America's most beautiful . . . Combines a vaguely aristocratic flavor with wahoo support of ACC athletic teams . . . Strong fraternity system rules campus social life.

University of Washington. The Pacific Northwest's leading research university . . . Strong across the board in pre-professional areas . . . In-staters constitute 90 percent of the student body at U-Dub . . . Admission difficult for out-of-staters . . . Currently grappling with budget cuts.

College of William and Mary. Often mistaken for a private liberal arts college ... In fact, it is a middle-size (8,000) public university ... Colonial Williamsburg campus steeped in history ... Out-of-state admission standards almost as high as those of UVA.

University of Wisconsin/Madison. Rivals University of Michigan as the upper Midwest's leading research university ... Strong distribution requirements ensure that all graduates are well rounded ... Strengths include the biological sciences, communications, and environmental studies.

Small-College Bargains

Here is a list for everyone who thought it was necessary to attend a behemoth state university to get an education at a bargain price. Most of the schools on this list are a different breed of cat: the public liberal arts colleges. In many ways, they resemble their private counterparts, offering small classes, a strong sense of community, and undivided attention to the liberal arts. The only difference is the price tag: out-of-state students can count on paying 30 to 50 percent less than at a private college, while in-staters will pocket enough savings to get a good start on graduate school— or that new BMW they've been wanting. New College of South Florida is the consensus leader in this category, but the others are gaining momentum.

In addition to the public liberal arts colleges, we include four private bargains.

Berea College. Absolutely tuition-free for students willing to work ten hours per week on campus ... The hitch: only needy students can attend this private institution ... Christian orientation fosters a strong sense of community and mission work ... Most students come from Kentucky and adjacent states.

Cooper Union for the Advancement of Science and Art. In the heart of Manhattan, a small private school (1,100) specializing in art, architecture, and engineering ... Founded by a philanthropist as a tuition-free school ... Campus consists of East Greenwich Village ... Acceptance rate lower than most Ivy League schools.

The Evergreen State College. This liberal haven in Olympia, Washington, is near the top of the budget list in the no-nonsense nineties ...

Also strong in one of the hot academic subjects of the nineties: environmental science . . . Attracts a large number of older "alternative" students.

Hendrix College. Tiny Hendrix (1,000) is a one of the most economical private liberal arts college in the nation . . . Tuition is half that charged by most Northeastern schools . . . Remote Arkansas location belies strong international emphasis . . . An unusually open and accepting community.

Mary Washington College. Easily mistaken for one of Virginia's elite private colleges . . . Offers as much history and tradition but at a lower price . . . Formerly the women's branch of UVA, now coed . . . Growing in reputation and selectivity.

University of Minnesota/Morris. If you've ever taken a wrong turn on the way to Duluth, you might have stumbled upon one of the best public liberal arts colleges in the country . . . Morris combines superb students, small classes, dedicated faculty, and an isolated prairie location.

New College of the University of South Florida. Elite liberal arts education at a bargain price . . . Largely independent of USF, which is 50 miles away in Tampa . . . Tiny student body (500) tends to be predominantly liberal . . . Beautiful waterfront campus.

University of North Carolina/Asheville. Medium-size (3,000) liberal arts college set in a Blue Ridge Mountain tourist hub . . . Especially strong in the natural sciences . . . More than 90 percent of the students are in-staters . . . Surrounding area is an outdoor enthusiast's paradise.

College of the Ozarks. A Missouri version of Berea . . . No tuition at this private institution, but family income must be low (approximately $30,000) to qualify for admission . . . Work requirements include fifteen hours a week plus additional hours during school vacations . . . Conservative in outlook and requires attendance at religious services.

St. Mary's College of Maryland. Often mistaken for a Catholic-affiliated school . . . Founded as a seminary for women, now a highly selective public college that is rapidly growing in popularity . . . Small student body (1,500) makes for close student-faculty relations . . . Strategically located one hour from both Washington, D.C., and Baltimore.

☞**See Also**

Morehouse College (Historically Black Colleges and Universities)
Spelman College (Historically Black Colleges and Universities)

PUBLIC UNIVERSITIES: THE HONORS PROGRAMS

The last in our triad of ways to beat the high cost of higher education is to attend an honors program at a state university. In the past decade or so, it has become a very "in" thing at large public universities to lavish attention and resources on a select group of handpicked students. By offering the combination of small classes, low tuition, and various other perks, these colleges hope to lure away some of the best and brightest from private universities that cost thousands more. At their best, these programs can be a great way to get a small-college education while enjoying all the benefits of a large university.

Aside from the particulars of the programs themselves, it is important to find out the relationship of the honors program to the university as a whole. Does the honors program have a critical mass of students? Or will you be dragged down to the prevailing mediocrity of the university as whole? Most important: Is the honors program perceived as an enclave of nerds who are uncool because they study too much? If so, you could be headed for a repeat of high school, something most intelligent students will want to avoid.

Almost any good university will have an honors program, many of them offering an education on a par with the most elite universities in the nation. Rather than attempting to be comprehensive, the following list includes only three that are among the very best in the nation.

University of Michigan/Ann Arbor/Residential College. In all probability, the best honors program in the universe . . . An elite student body of 950 lives and works in the same residential college . . . All classes are taught in seminar format . . . Generally attracts students with leftist, artsy leanings.

University of Texas/Austin/Plan II. A highly selective program that includes small seminars, top faculty, and a wide variety of enrichment experiences . . . Given UT's bargain-basement price, this program is probably the single best buy in all of higher education . . . Limited to approximately 700 students.

University of Virginia/Echols Scholars Program. About 800 of UVA's most elite get the Echols designation . . . Students are given complete freedom to design their own academic programs . . . All Echols students are housed together in the freshman year.

OTHER EXCELLENT SMALL COLLEGES

This list reflects the reality that there are many more good small colleges for undergraduate study than there are good large universities. For every mega-university with 20,000 undergraduates, there are ten small colleges with 2,000 students that are probably superior in most respects.

The colleges on this list are a diverse lot, but all have a total enrollment of under 4,000. Most have no graduate students at all. The rest have a smattering of them but are still mainly undergraduate institutions. If you're looking for a college and don't find it here, check out some of the other lists. There are many more excellent small colleges that we have chosen to classify by a particular trait.

Allegheny College. Pennsylvania liberal arts college with a down-to-earth Midwestern flavor . . . Strong science programs benefit from superb facilities . . . Student body is less affluent than at competitors such as Dickinson and Bucknell . . . Football team usually contends for the Division 111 national championship.

Beloit College. Tiny Midwestern college (1,200) known for free-thinking students and international focus . . . Has steered back toward the mainstream after its heyday as an alternative school in the sixties and seventies . . . Wisconsin location makes Beloit easier to get into than similar Northeastern schools.

Bucknell University. Very selective "near Ivy" that attracts conservative, career-oriented students . . . Central Pennsylvania campus is isolated but among the most picturesque in the nation . . . Strong fraternity and sorority system offers traditional college social life . . . Administration working to expand diversity.

Brandeis University. Prestigious Massachusetts college founded fifty years ago under Jewish auspices . . . Student body is two-thirds Jewish, but campus flavor closely resembles other Northeastern schools . . . Academic specialties include the natural sciences, the Middle East, and Jewish Studies . . . Modern buildings lack traditional "feel."

Claremont McKenna College. Small California liberal arts college dedicated to business and politics . . . Benefits enormously from close ties to the four other Claremont Colleges . . . Formerly Claremont Men's College, and still almost two-thirds male.

Clark University. Small university (2,900) that offers unique opportunities for undergraduate research . . . Often overshadowed by the Boston schools one hour to the east . . . World-famous in psychology and geography . . . Easier in admissions than many other schools of similar quality.

Colgate University. Front runner of the upstate New York liberal arts colleges . . . Attracts an outdoorsy, athletic student body . . . Fraternities and sororities still well entrenched despite the college's efforts to neutralize them . . . The most selective school on this list.

Colorado College. Under its "Block Plan," students study one course at a time in month-long segments . . . Great for science labs, in-depth study, field trips . . . Less well suited to assignments that take more than a month . . . Colorado Springs provides easy access to Rocky Mountain playlands.

Connecticut College. Pioneer in successful transition from women's college to coed . . . Seemingly everyone has good things to say about Conn Coll . . . Recently made SAT I optional for admission . . . Among the best study-abroad programs in the nation.

Denison University. Working hard to create a more serious academic atmosphere . . . Recently closed fraternity and sorority houses in an attempt to diversify the social climate . . . Though located in Ohio, Denison draws a significant percentage of students from the Northeast.

Dickinson College. Historic small college in the foothills of central Pennsylvania . . . Operates numerous study-abroad programs and emphasizes foreign languages . . . Known for interdisciplinary programs . . . Competes with the elite but is often a second choice.

Drew University. Tiny New Jersey university (2,000) with an attractive wooded campus . . . Strong political science program places interns at the United Nations . . . Half an hour by train to the Big Apple . . . Still in search of a national identity.

Franklin and Marshall College. Eastern Pennsylvania school known for pre-professional students and a pipeline of internships to Capitol Hill . . . Common aspirations to law, medicine, and business create a hard-working and competitive atmosphere.

Gettysburg College. Another central Pennsylvania liberal arts college often associated with Dickinson and with Franklin and Marshall . . . Nearby Civil War battlefield helps make the history department one of the best and most popular . . . Strong fraternity-and-sorority system includes about one-half of the students.

Gustavus Adolphus College. Named for a seventeenth-century Swedish King who defended Lutheranism against the Catholics . . . Two-thirds of the students are members of the faith, and most are homegrown Minnesotans . . . Strong core requirements ensure broad exposure to the liberal arts . . . Offers unusual opportunities for undergraduate research.

Hamilton College. Once a conservative men's college, Hamilton became coed in 1978 when it swallowed artsy Kirkland College . . . The marriage has ensured more diversity and strength across the curriculum . . . Set on an opulent rural upstate New York campus . . . Fights uphill battle for students in competition with schools in the Elite category.

Hobart and William Smith Colleges. Coordinate single-sex colleges overlooking one of New York's Finger Lakes . . . Each college has its own administration on formerly separate campuses . . . Fraternities and men's lacrosse dominate the traditional social scene . . . Geneva is a rusting industrial town.

Lafayette College. Close kin to Colgate, Hamilton, and Bucknell . . . Provides highly competitive academic climate and traditional college experience . . . One of the few small liberal arts colleges that offer engineering . . . Social life revolves around fraternities and sororities.

Lake Forest College. Tiny school (1,000) that occupies an exclusive enclave on Lake Michigan north of Chicago . . . Students tend to be clean-cut and affluent . . . Well-developed internship program lets Foresters get full-time real-world experience . . . Commuter railway provides easy access to Chicago.

Lawrence University. Underrated Wisconsin college combining the liberal arts with one of the best music conservatories in the nation . . . Despite the word "university" in its name, Lawrence is really a very small college (1,200) . . . Another top Midwest liberal arts college that would be much more selective if on the East Coast.

Lewis and Clark College. Close second to Reed for the title of best Pacific Northwest liberal arts college . . . Known for international affairs and the fact that the whole student body does at least one semester of study abroad . . . Admissions office allows students to bypass standardized test scores if they choose . . . Located in affluent suburban Portland.

Occidental College. One of the nation's few small colleges located in a major city (Los Angeles) . . . Strong international focus (especially Hispanic) and trimester system ideal for study abroad . . . A new initiative seeks to attract more minorities and integrate more fully with the city.

Ohio Wesleyan University. Often mentioned in the same breath with Denison . . . A bit more Midwestern, a bit less preppy than its nearby counterpart . . . As at Denison, the administration is doing its best to put the clamps on the Greek system and raise academic standards . . . Students tend to be mainstream and career-oriented.

Rhodes College. One of the best liberal arts colleges in the South . . . Often compared to the University of the South (Sewanee), Rhodes is the more progressive of the two . . . Formerly called Southwestern at Memphis . . . Wins prize for best student nickname: Rhodents.

St. John's College. Unique small college known for its great-books curriculum and its dual campuses in Maryland and New Mexico . . . From the ancient Greeks to Einstein, most subjects are taught from 150 classics of the Western tradition . . . Professors are viewed as "tutors" and fellow students of the classics.

St. Lawrence University. Liberal arts outpost in the northernmost reaches of New York State . . . Surrounded by wilderness and strong in "hot" environmental studies area . . . A conventional student body with a streak of outdoorsy nonconformity.

Skidmore College. A former women's college with artistic flair . . . Bolstered by new facilities, the creative and performing arts set the tone of campus . . . Forested campus is among the most secluded and peaceful in the nation . . . Located on the outskirts of Saratoga Springs, a nineteenth-century upstate New York resort.

University of the South (Sewanee). This small (1,200) Central Tennessee liberal arts college is just the sort of place that its name implies . . . Regal 10,000-acre campus with stately neo-Gothic architecture . . . Voluntary dress code includes skirts for women and jacket and tie for men . . . Especially noted for its English department.

Trinity College (Connecticut). One of the Northeast's few urban liberal arts colleges . . . Competes with the Elite for students but is often a second choice . . . Operates extensive internship and study-abroad programs . . . The campus is a beautiful oasis in an iffy urban neighborhood.

Union College. Unusual combination of engineering and the liberal arts in a small (2,100) school . . . Even the engineers take a five-course sequence in Western Civ. . . . Trimester calendar makes for abundant internships and opportunities for study abroad . . . Strong Greek system defines the social scene.

Vassar College. Former Seven Sister that retains avant-garde flair . . . Now coed, Vassar is especially strong in the humanities and social sciences . . . Political views somewhere between liberal and very, very liberal . . . Gorgeous campus on the edge of blue-collar Poughkeepsie.

Washington and Lee University. The ideal of the gentleman scholar (now gentleperson scholar) is alive and well at W&L . . . Went coed in the mid-eighties after an emotional debate but still 60 percent male . . . Noted for geographic diversity, social science programs, and conservative students . . . One of the South's most prestigious liberal arts colleges.

Wheaton College (Massachusetts). One of the last of the prestigious women's colleges to opt for coeducation . . . Beautiful campus and strategic location one half hour from Boston . . . Two-to-one ratio of females to males makes social life a bit awkward for the women.

Wofford College. Tiny South Carolina college (1,100) that serves mainly in-staters . . . Low tuition places it among the private college bargains . . . Offers strong programs in the humanities, natural sciences, and business . . . Social life is dominated by fraternities.

College of Wooster. Widely renowned in academic circles, Wooster is less known to the general public . . . Easy to get in, harder to graduate . . . All students complete an independent study project in their junior and senior years . . . Intellectually serious and international in outlook.

OTHER WELL-KNOWN UNIVERSITIES

The universities on this list attract many top students but are not quite as choosy as the Elite. Each of them has its own specialties, usually in pre-professional areas. Self-starters who have a particular program in mind will be well served.

Liberal arts students should go in with both eyes open. As with large public universities, an honors program would be a good bet. The main priority is to avoid getting lost in the crowd.

Enrollments at these universities range from 4,200 to 36,500, placing them in the medium-to-large category. Most are private universities, though the list includes two premier public universities (Michigan and Vermont) that no longer qualify for bargain status because of hefty out-of-state tuition. Finally, each school on this list is located in or near a major city.

The American University. Suburban D.C. location sets the tone for this middle-size (11,700) university . . . Drawing cards include politics, economics, communications, and international relations . . . Host role for the Washington Semester program ensures a steady influx of new faces . . . Lively Georgetown party scene does major damage to GPAs.

Boston University. Huge private university (28,600) in the bustling Back Bay . . . Best known for pre-med, communications, engineering, and the arts . . . Honors programs are the best bet in the liberal arts . . . Traditionalist administration alienates some students and faculty.

Carnegie Mellon University. Unique in its combination of top technology programs with equally strong arts programs . . . Among the nation's leaders in the integration of computers across the curriculum . . . Academic climate unusually intense . . . Admissions standards vary widely, depending on the program.

University of Denver. Middle-size university known equally for business and skiing . . . Laid-back atmosphere prevails . . . Campus in residential Denver is pleasant but not inspiring . . . Students tend to be outdoorsy and environmentally conscious.

George Washington University. Strategic D.C. location within a stone's throw of the White House . . . Strong in anything related to politics and economics . . . No campus and little sense of community . . . Similar to American U. except for downtown location.

Lehigh University. Combines top business and engineering programs in a middle-size university (6,500) . . . The arts and sciences are better than at most technically oriented schools . . . Greek system rules social life . . . Nice hillside campus, though Bethlehem has little to offer.

University of Massachusetts/Amherst. Liberal Mecca in cosmopolitan and scenic Western Massachusetts . . . Strong study-abroad programs add international flavor . . . Strong ties to Amherst, Hampshire, Mount Holyoke, and Smith via the Five College Consortium.

University of Michigan. The most interesting mass of humanity east of UC/Berkeley . . . Among the nation's best in most subjects, but undergraduates must elbow their way to the front to get full benefit . . . Superb honors programs are the best bet for highly motivated students.

New York University. Located smack in the middle of Greenwich Village . . . World-renowned programs in the arts and media, and also strong in business . . . No campus except for Washington Square Park . . . The ultimate "sink-or-swim" school.

University of Richmond. Small Virginia university (4,200) with growing appeal among conservative, affluent Easterners . . . Has the nation's first School of Leadership Studies in addition to business and arts and sciences . . . Secluded edge-of-town campus . . . Men's and women's dorms separated by a pond.

University of Southern California. A more expensive alternative to the University of California system . . . Best bets include the honors program, business, or nationally acclaimed offerings in the arts or cinema/TV . . . Iffy L.A. neighborhood means crime is always a concern.

Southern Methodist University. A private (and much more expensive) alternative to the University of Texas . . . SMU's renowned School of the Arts is among the finest in the nation . . . Predominantly conservative student body flocks to the business program . . . Posh suburban campus assures a comfortable four years.

Syracuse University. A big school (14,500) that has renewed its commitment to undergraduate teaching . . . Famous for professional schools, notably communications and public affairs . . . Standards in the arts and sciences are less stringent . . . Set on a hill overlooking downtown.

Tulane University. Though located in New Orleans, Tulane is as popular among Yankees as it is among Southerners . . . Close cousin to Emory, though less selective . . . Offers respected programs in architecture, business, engineering, and the liberal arts . . . Bustling social life includes the French Quarter and Mardi Gras.

University of Vermont. Medium-size public university (8,000) that feels like a private college . . . Superb Burlington location combines easy access to natural wonders while offering college-town ambience . . . Half the students are out-of-staters.

☞ See Also

For other lists that include well-known universities, see Historically Black Colleges and Universities, The Roman Catholic World, and Top Conservative Colleges.

THE BEST-KEPT SECRETS

No flashy window decals here. Though the colleges listed here are well known in their respective states, on the national level they are largely anonymous outside of a few devoted alumni and graduate school admissions officers. The latter group, however, is an important one. Rest assured that a degree from any of these colleges will get the respect it deserves when the time comes to apply to law school, medical school, or any other kind of school. As for the window decal, think of it as a well-kept secret—only a select few will recognize its significance.

Alfred University. Rare hybrid that includes excellent liberal arts and nationally known art and design programs . . . Includes the country's premier ceramic engineering program . . . Rural location in the Finger Lakes of upstate New York . . . Total enrollment 2,500.

Centre College. Small Kentucky college (1,000) known for producing Rhodes Scholars and devoted alumni . . . Traditional liberal arts curriculum, largely conservative student body . . . Fraternities and football games are the staples of social life . . . Old grads still reminisce about gridiron upset of Harvard in 1921.

Eckerd College. Small Florida college (1,400) best known for marine biology . . . Combines strong sense of community with liberal, open-minded atmosphere . . . No fraternities or sororities . . . Gorgeous St. Petersburg campus overlooks the Gulf of Mexico.

Guilford College. One of the few Quaker schools in the South . . . Emphasizes a collaborative approach to all phases of life . . . One of the most liberal student bodies in the South . . . Offers strong study-abroad programs . . . Central North Carolina location is within easy reach of the Duke–UNC–NC State research triangle.

Hiram College. Tiny Ohio college (900) offering strong community spirit and top-notch biology program . . . Ecology research station adjoins the campus . . . All-American, friendly, middle-of-the-road student body . . . Offers Midwest tranquillity, with Cleveland about one hour's drive away.

Illinois Wesleyan University. Up-and-coming small university (1,800) in Middle America . . . Eighty percent of the students are Illinois natives . . . Strong in fine arts and pre-anything . . . Methodist affiliation is low-key . . . Recent construction includes new gym and state-of-the-art science facility.

Knox College. Target of relentless "School of Hard Knox" jokes . . . Friendly, progressive Illinois college that was among the first in the nation to admit blacks and women . . . Offers close interaction with faculty and pure liberal arts . . . Located amid cornfields midway between Chicago and St. Louis . . . Very small (1,000).

Millsaps College. The pride of Mississippi higher education . . . Best liberal arts college in the Deep, Deep South . . . Largely pre-professional student body has sights set on business, law, and medicine . . . Known as liberal hotbed in Mississippi (translation: middle-of-the-road to conservative).

Presbyterian College. Small South Carolina college (1,100) with a big endowment . . . Despite the name, only about a third of the students are

Presbyterians . . . Extensive core curriculum covers the liberal arts . . . Struggling to attract more minorities.

University of Puget Sound. One of a trio of colleges in the Pacific Northwest (along with Whitman and Willamette) that deserve more national exposure . . . Tacoma campus features easy access to Puget Sound and Mount Rainier . . . Best known for Asian studies and study-abroad programs.

University of Redlands. One of the West Coast's most versatile small colleges (1,500) . . . Offers optional individualized program in which students "contract" with faculty to create their entire program . . . Also offers pre-professional training in business, education, and even engineering.

Whitman College. Small college (1,200) tucked away in beautiful eastern Washington State . . . Traditional liberal arts curriculum served up with abundant personal attention . . . Hiking, biking, rock climbing, and white-water rafting all within easy reach.

Willamette University. Despite the name, Willamette is a small college (2,500) with a few hundred graduate students . . . Adjacent Oregon state capitol bolsters economics and political science offerings . . . Unusually strong study-abroad programs.

Wittenberg University. Friendly Ohio campus that sparks intense loyalty among students and alumni . . . Has an All-American, heartland flavor . . . Strong school spirit, strong athletic teams . . . Springfield is a small city thirty minutes from Dayton.

☞**See Also**

Small-College Bargains

TOP WOMEN'S COLLEGES

It's been a long, strange trip for the nation's women's colleges since the coeducation movement of the late sixties. First, there was much hand-wringing and talk of admitting men or even pulling up stakes to move the entire college to join a counterpart male school hundreds of miles away. By 1980, it looked as if women's colleges might one day go the way of leisure suits and eight-track tapes. Then came the discovery that coed schools might not be such a great place for women after all, with classrooms dominated by male counterparts. Study after study detailing "how coed colleges cheat women" saturated the education journals, and suddenly women's colleges were riding high. Today, the long-term future of women's colleges seems secure, regardless of the next twist in the gender wars.

History lesson aside, women's colleges are looking like a good bet for today's talented young women. With a higher percentage of women on their faculties than coed schools, these colleges offer abundant role models who are committed to helping women reach their full potential. The case is strongest in the sciences, where the evidence is clear that these schools do a better job of turning out female scientists than their coed counterparts. No matter what they study, students cite a sense of acceptance and sisterly camaraderie. Meanwhile, the high point of the week at most coed schools is watching male warriors strut around a stadium and beat each other's brains out while women cheerlead.

One myth about women's colleges desperately needs debunking: that they are best for shy, wallflowerish types too delicate to rub shoulders with men. On the contrary, the students who choose women's colleges tend to be confident, outgoing, and self-reliant. When they want to be with men, they know how to find them.

Last, a strategic note. Most of these colleges are not quite as competitive in admissions as they were before coeducation. It stands to reason: the coed schools have gobbled up a significant slice of their market. But that creates an opportunity for other young women who might not have had the opportunity twenty years ago. After all, these colleges are still among the oldest, richest, and all-round best in the nation.

Below is a selection of what we think are some of the top women's colleges in the nation. We have included only those that have a significant degree of autonomy from parent universities or coordinate all-male institutions.

Agnes Scott College. Tiny Atlanta college with big bucks in its endowment . . . The 600-woman student body creates unparalleled sense of community among students and faculty . . . Secluded suburban campus in the leading city of the Southeast . . . Social life dependent primarily on Georgia Tech frat parties.

Barnard College. Boldly asserted its independence by refusing closer ties to brother school Columbia College in the early eighties . . . All the resources of Columbia University and New York City at its finger-tips . . . Barnard women generally more liberal, artsy, and into the City than their Columbia counterparts . . . Small-towners should be crystal-clear on what they're getting into.

Hollins College. Traditional women's college in southwest Virginia . . . Main strengths lie in the humanities and social sciences . . . Creative writing is a specialty . . . Social life revolves around frat parties at nearby coed schools, such as Washington and Lee and Virginia Tech.

Mills College. Best known for the firestorm of protest that torpedoed a 1990 Board of Trustees proposal to go coed . . . Problems remain, but enrollment has inched upward since the decision to stay all-female . . . One of the few all-female options on the West Coast . . . UC/Berkeley and San Francisco are both within easy reach of Oakland campus.

Mount Holyoke College. One of the most prosperous of the elite women's colleges . . . Ideal western Massachusetts location . . . Combines strong sense of community with abundant opportunities from Five-College Consortium (Amherst, Hampshire, UMass/Amherst, Smith) . . . Particularly strong in the natural sciences.

Randolph-Macon Woman's College. Traditionally known as the most academic of the Virginia women's colleges . . . Not to be confused with the coed Randolph-Macon north of Richmond . . . Rightly proud of its attention to each individual and the close relations between students and faculty . . . Male companionship from Hampden-Sydney, Washington and Lee, and UVA.

Scripps College. Tiny women's college (600) that is part of the Claremont consortium (with Harvey Mudd, Claremont McKenna, Pitzer, and Pomona) . . . English and the humanities top the list of strong departments . . . Near L.A. . . . Scripps offers an ideal climate when not shrouded in smog.

Smith College. Like a slice of Greenwich Village plunked down in western Massachusetts . . . More liberal than its counterparts Wellesley and Mount Holyoke . . . Chic Northampton is a mecca for the gay community . . . Five-College Consortium (Amherst, Hampshire, UMass/Amherst, and Mount Holyoke) offers enormous range of opportunities.

Sweet Briar College. Historically a sanctuary for Southern belles . . . Today's students are more career-oriented but still very traditional in outlook . . . Rural Virginia location is picturesque, if isolated . . . Traditional triad of Hampden-Sydney, Washington and Lee, and UVA provide the primary male companionship.

Wells College. Tiny school (400) on the shores of the Finger Lakes in upstate New York . . . Tight-knit community offers unusually close student-faculty interactions . . . Single dinner bell rings for the evening meal . . . Students offered abundant opportunity to design their own curriculum, but is there a critical mass of courses?

☞**See Also**

> **Bryn Mawr College** (The Elite Liberal Arts Colleges)
> **Spelman College** (Historically Black Colleges and Universities)
> **Wellesley College** (The Elite Liberal Arts Colleges)

TOP HISTORICALLY BLACK COLLEGES AND UNIVERSITIES

Historically black colleges date from the time when African Americans were denied access to predominantly white institutions. There are approximately one hundred historically black schools in the nation, the majority of which are located in the Southeast. They are generally less selective, less wealthy, and less prestigious (in white America) than the colleges we have listed so far. Now that the latter are standing in line to recruit talented minority students, is there any reason to consider a historically black school?

In many cases, the answer is yes. From Jesse Jackson to Spike Lee, a high percentage of the nation's most prominent African Americans attended a black college. Though often strapped for cash, the colleges offer things money can't buy: relief from the constant burden of minority status, a chance to study the black experience as a central focus, and closer relationships with faculty and fellow students. Involvement in the community is an important predictor of success in college, which is one reason for higher graduation rates among students at black colleges than blacks at mainstream schools. Though predominantly white schools often roll out the red carpet for minorities during the admissions process, they seldom maintain the same level of attention after enrollment. No matter how much administrators preach about diversity, the "black community" at many such schools is confined to the fringes of campus life. Though historically black schools are not household names, they continue to pay dividends after graduation. Most have intensely loyal alumni who will go out of their way to help a fellow graduate.

One of the myths about historically black colleges is that they cater to students who would have difficulty functioning in white America. In fact, such schools are often most valuable for those who grew up as the only black face in a white crowd. For these students, a historically black college may offer the only chance in their lifetime to live and learn in a community of fellow African Americans.

One final virtue these colleges offer: a bargain price. Along with the public liberal arts colleges, historically black schools give the most for the money of any category in this chapter.

Clark Atlanta University. The university at the core of the Atlanta University Center, the national focal point of historically black education . . . Benefits from coordinate relationship with prestigious Morehouse and Spelman Colleges . . . Strong in business, communications, health professions, and public policy.

Florida A&M University. Public university best known for business, engineering, and journalism . . . Shares state capital Tallahassee with Florida State University . . . With an enrollment of nearly 10,000, it is one of the largest historically black universities in the nation.

Hampton University. One of the best endowed historically black colleges and also one of the most selective . . . Best known for its business school . . . Located on the Virginia coast near Norfolk . . . Hampton attracts students from both sides of the Mason-Dixon line.

Howard University. The nation's most famous historically black university . . . Pioneer of the Afrocentric approach to learning across the curriculum . . . Has recently weathered financial difficulties that forced cuts in administration and staff . . . Location in Washington, D.C., is ideal for politics and economics.

Lincoln University (Pennsylvania). Founded in 1854, this is the nation's oldest historically black university . . . Alma mater of Supreme Court Justice Thurgood Marshall and poet Langston Hughes . . . Southeastern Pennsylvania location seems isolated to city dwellers.

Morehouse College. Along with sister school Spelman, the most selective of the historically black schools . . . Alma mater to some of the most prominent black men in American history, notably the Rev. Martin Luther King, Jr. . . . Best known for business and popular 3–2 engineering program with Georgia Tech.

Morgan State University.   Next to Howard and Hampton, one of the best-known historically black universities in the Middle Atlantic states . . . Known for business and strong sports teams . . . Located in Baltimore.

Spelman College.   Sister school to Morehouse . . . The richest of the historically black colleges, thanks to a recent $20 million gift from the Bill Cosby family . . . Strong liberal arts focus, with English and psychology the most popular majors . . . Wooded Atlanta campus provides easy access to urban attractions.

Tuskegee University.   Formerly Tuskegee Institute . . . Historically committed to pre-professional training rather than the study of black culture . . . Strongest in engineering, with pre-med and business also popular . . . Isolated central Alabama location.

Xavier University (Louisiana).   Small Louisiana school with a big reputation for producing successful scientists . . . The nation's only black Roman Catholic–affiliated institution . . . Women outnumber men by two to one . . . Bustling location in downtown New Orleans.

THE ROMAN CATHOLIC WORLD

The Roman Catholic–affiliated schools are a distinctive segment of the higher-education scene. The advantages to a Catholic student include a strong sense of community, shared values, and a traditional social life (though often without Greek letter fraternities). On the other hand, some students will feel confined by the relative lack of diversity and the "sheep following the herd" mentality that sometimes creeps into the culture.

Catholic schools tend to be traditional in their approach to academics. In the arts and sciences, most have a core curriculum or similar structured approach that accents the Western tradition. These schools also tend to have a strong pre-professional emphasis.

The schools vary in the extent to which religion sets the tone of campus life. Technically, most are affiliated not with the church itself but with a particular order, such as the Jesuits or the Franciscans. At some, the Catholic religion is barely noticeable except for the fact that the president wears a Roman collar. At others, clergy hold key administrative positions, religion courses are required, monks live in the dorms, and daily mass is a foregone conclusion. A good index of "how Catholic" is the percentage of students who belong to the faith. The range is from about 50 percent to 90 percent.

Boston College. Enjoys booming national popularity among all faiths because of athletic teams and prime Boston location . . . Comfortable home for students who want a good name and good partying, but popularity appears out of proportion to quality . . . Enrollment 80 percent Catholic . . . Now a close second to Notre Dame in the pecking order among true-blue Catholics.

The Catholic University of America. The only university in the nation that is chartered by the Vatican . . . Enrollment 90 percent Catholic . . . Clergy constitute only 10 percent of arts and sciences faculty, but campus tone is more strictly Catholic than most other schools on this list.

University of Dallas. Without a doubt the best Catholic-affiliated college south of Washington, D.C. . . . Only 1,000 undergraduates, lots of attention from faculty, and curriculum emphasizing the Western tradition . . . Enrollment 70 percent Catholic . . . Unlike many Catholic-affiliated schools, intercollegiate athletics are deemphasized . . . Large endowment makes future bright.

DePaul University. Gets the nod over Loyola as the best Catholic university in Chicago . . . Lincoln Park location is like New York's Greenwich Village or Upper West Side without all the headaches . . . Student body largely a feeder to Chicago's business community . . . Almost half non-Catholic . . . Robust enrollment increases bode well for the future.

Fairfield University. One of the up-and-coming schools in the Catholic universe . . . Strategic Connecticut location and ready access to New York City are two major assets . . . Undergraduate enrollment of 3,000 makes FU smaller than many of its competitors . . . Little known outside the Northeast . . . Enrollment 90 percent Catholic.

College of the Holy Cross. Small, tight-knit Catholic community steeped in church and tradition . . . Enrollment overwhelmingly New

England Irish descent . . . Many students are second or third generation to attend . . . Though gritty, Worcester is an hour from Boston and home to nine other colleges.

John Carroll University. Although named "University," JC is really a small college (3,000 students) that is acquiring a big reputation in the Midwest . . . Occupies scenic enclave in Cleveland's exclusive eastern suburbs . . . Enrollment 70 percent Catholic . . . Many have aspirations toward the Cleveland-area business community.

Marquette University. Best known as a second choice to Notre Dame . . . Strong programs include engineering, health professions, and business . . . Downtown campus in so-so neighborhood blends well with Milwaukee's working-class aura . . . About 80 percent of the campus is Catholic.

University of Notre Dame. The Holy Grail of higher ed for many Catholics . . . Heartland location and 90 percent Catholic enrollment help make ND a bastion of traditional values . . . Lack of fraternities doesn't dampen party scene . . . Football coach second only to Jesus in approval rating.

Saint Louis University. One of the heartland's few Catholic universities . . . A standout in the health professions . . . Located downtown near the Gateway Arch in the city's West End . . . With no football team, SLU is a soccer powerhouse.

University of San Francisco. Middle-sized institution in the heart of San Francisco, overlooking the city skyline . . . Liberal city, conservative school make for interesting mix . . . West Coast location gives student body more diversity than similar universities in the East . . . Approximately half the students are Catholic.

Santa Clara University. Probably the best Catholic-affiliated school west of the Rockies . . . Gorgeous Silicon Valley campus is within easy reach of San Francisco . . . Large endowment also contributes to air of prosperity . . . About 60 percent of the student body is Catholic.

Villanova University. Middle-sized Philadelphia university with a more upscale image than some of its competitors . . . Located in the affluent Main Line suburbs near Haverford and Bryn Mawr . . . Big East basketball is main excitement on campus . . . About 85 percent of the students are Catholic.

☞See Also

Alverno College (The Most Innovative Curriculums)
Georgetown University (The Elite Private Universities)
Xavier University (Louisiana) (Historically Black Colleges and Universities)

TOP CONSERVATIVE COLLEGES

There are many reasons why students and parents would want to consider a conservative college. Let's face it, the political climate at most elite liberal arts colleges is dominated by liberals. Even at schools where conservatives may constitute a "silent majority," they are often reluctant to challenge the prevailing "political correctness." Furthermore, university faculties are overwhelmingly liberal, almost without exception in arts-and-sciences schools. In recent years, the gap between the values of college faculties and the more conservative segments of society has grown increasingly wide. Many families may be seeking one or more of the following:

- a place that emphasizes the Western tradition rather than multiculturalism
- a place where conservative opinions can be openly expressed without being branded as racist or sexist
- a place where moral and/or Christian values set the tenor of life

Obviously, any attempt at a comprehensive listing of such colleges would be impossible. The term "conservative" is itself a broad generalization that encompasses a wide array of values and beliefs. To paraphrase the *Fiske Guide to Colleges*, we offer this diverse list as a selection of the "best and most interesting" schools that tend toward a conservative perspective.

One pattern you'll probably notice right away: Most of the schools on this list are in the South. With few exceptions, colleges in the South are more conservative in a host of ways than their counterparts in the Northeast and Midwest (the West Coast is a mixed bag). Students seeking more of the traditional trappings of college life may want to look at some Southern colleges. Note as well that most of the colleges on the Catholic-affiliated list would also fit here.

Babson College. Boston-area school that is devoted exclusively to business . . . Offers highly touted Entrepreneurial Studies program . . . Men outnumber women by almost two to one . . . One of the few conservative outposts in liberal Massachusetts.

Birmingham-Southern College. One of the Deep South's best liberal arts colleges . . . The vast majority of students come from Alabama and the surrounding states . . . Strong fraternity system . . . A throwback to the way college used to be.

Brigham Young University. The flagship university of Mormonism . . . Visitors will find an endless sea of clean-cut, all-American students (27,000 undergraduates) . . . Most men and some women do a two-year stint as a missionary . . . Mild-mannered campus goes bonkers for sports teams.

Calvin College. Evangelical Christian school that ranks high on the private-college bargain list . . . Over half the students are members of the Christian Reformed Church . . . Particularly strong in the humanities . . . Archrival of Michigan neighbor Hope College.

DePauw University. Small Indiana college that has helped populate the Indiana business and government elite . . . Making major strides in attracting more minorities . . . One of the strongest fraternity systems in the nation . . . Trying to live down association with its most famous alum, former VP Dan Quayle.

George Mason University. Capitalizing, so to speak, on proximity to Washington, D.C. . . . Leading center of conservative political and economic thought . . . Once a sleepy commuter school, now challenging UVA and Virginia Tech in many fields for primacy among Virginia state schools.

Grove City College. A rising star among conservative colleges . . . Known for refusal to accept government funds . . . Low tuition translates to a top rating among bargain schools . . . Christian values set the tone . . . Small-town campus is within striking distance of Pittsburgh.

Hampden-Sydney College. Southern Virginia conservative bastion that is one of two all-male liberal arts colleges left in the nation . . . Feeder school to the Virginia political and economic establishment in Richmond . . . Picturesque eastern Virginia setting where the Old South still lives.

Hope College. Small Christian school (2,800) that is best known for its programs in the natural sciences . . . Also strong in the arts and business . . . Located in a small city by the shores of Lake Michigan . . . Affiliated with the Dutch Reformed Church in America.

Pepperdine University. Opulent hillside paradise in L.A.'s ritzy Malibu . . . Within walking distance of the Pacific . . . Affiliation with Disciples of Christ means no drinking and strict visitation rules . . . Dancing now allowed . . . Business is by far the most popular program.

St. Olaf College. A Minnesota liberal arts college of Norwegian Lutheran persuasion . . . Known for traditional values, international studies, a world-class choir, and the blondest student body this side of Oslo . . . Shares the same small town with Carleton, another nationally known liberal arts college.

Trinity University (Texas). A liberal arts college that has been rolling in dough ever since the 1970s oil boom . . . Has used its money to lure a high-powered student body heavy on National Merit Scholars . . . Though middle-of-the-road by Texas standards, it is conservative by those of the rest of the country.

Wabash College. Last outpost of all-male higher education in the Midwest . . . Small size (800) and single-sex status make for unique camaraderie . . . Student body includes plenty of gentleman jocks and clean-cut future professionals . . . Huge endowment makes college's future secure.

Wheaton College (Illinois). The premier evangelical Christian school in the country . . . All students sign a pledge to abstain from vices ranging from alcohol to "occult practices" . . . School motto: "For Christ and His Kingdom" . . . Ranks high on list of bargain schools, with tuition thousands less than most liberal arts colleges.

☞**See Also**

The Roman Catholic World
Claremont McKenna College (Other Excellent Small Colleges)

Dartmouth College (The Elite Private Universities)
University of the South (Other Excellent Small Colleges)
University of Southern California (Other Well-Known Universities)
Vanderbilt University (Rising Stars)
Washington and Lee University (Other Excellent Small Colleges)

TOP NONCONFORMIST COLLEGES

Let's get one thing straight: These are not merely colleges with a somewhat liberal bent. Ted Kennedy is liberal. *The New York Times* is liberal. Many of the most selective colleges in the country have a mainstream liberal tenor.

These are places where students question the very foundations of what might be termed "the establishment" (though that doesn't mean they won't end up as doctors or lawyers someday). Many of the student bodies call to mind images of the 1960s: long hair, protest marches, communal-style living, and lots of kids who look like Grateful Dead groupies. At others, pink hair blends with purple combat boots and black leather to provide a bohemian, Greenwich Village ambience. Most of these campuses are known for individualism, and alternative lifestyles such as homosexuality are not merely tolerated but embraced. In exchange for increased independence, students lose the traditional trappings of college life—no football games, no fraternity pranks, and often, little sense of their collective identity. For most students at these colleges, that's no big loss.

By and large, the academic caliber of these places tends to be high. The act of questioning authority is generally a sign of intelligence in the young, and students at these colleges do more than their share. Virtually all of these colleges offer a nontraditional twist to the curriculum, and many are among the leaders in innovation across the curriculum. Elements may include self-designed majors, broad thematic courses, hands-on experiences, and de-emphasis of letter grades. Most of these colleges tend to be strongest in the arts and humanities, though science is a specialty at a few.

The downside of these schools is the fact that they are so far out of step with the mainstream of society in these more conservative times. A generation ago, a number of them were hot among legions of rebellious youth that numbered among the best and brightest. Today, most of these colleges are less selective than they once were, though interest seems to have rebounded somewhat in recent years. They also suffer, in varying degrees, from the blight of political correctness that stems from their lack of conservative and even moderate voices. Finally, they generally have far less endowment than their more mainstream cousins and often run on shoestring budgets.

Antioch College. One of the most alternative of the alternative schools . . . Specializes in term-time internships that give students real-world experience for academic credit . . . Has never fully recovered from near bankruptcy in the late 1970s.

Bard College. Hotbed of artsy intellectualism where the president is known simply as "Leon" . . . Recent mega-million-dollar gifts have put Bard on firm financial footing . . . Immediate Decision Plan gives students a shot at on-the-spot acceptance after an interview . . . Curriculum that emphasizes small classes, writing, and intense self-questioning . . . Picturesque Hudson Valley location is one hour by train from New York City.

Bennington College. Known for top-notch performing arts and lavish attention to every student . . . Recent financial and enrollment difficulties now under control . . . Now successfully reinventing itself with innovative use of part-time faculty who are practitioners in their fields . . . Picturesque location in the foothills of the Green Mountains.

University of California/Santa Cruz. One of the nation's best-known destinations for nonconformists . . . Part of the highly competitive University of California system, recently buffeted by budget cuts . . . Curriculum becoming increasingly traditional, as administration looks to change "alternative" label.

Earlham College. Small Indiana college (1,000) of Quaker origins . . . Similar in character to Oberlin and Grinnell, though slightly less selective . . . Strong ties to Japan accentuate international outlook . . . An alien presence in conservative southern Indiana.

Hampshire College. Child of the 1960s nestled in Massachusetts' prestigious Five-College Consortium . . . Best known for photography and film . . . Unique features include substantial individual projects and thematic approach that integrates traditional academic subjects.

Marlboro College. Hilltop home to 280 nonconformist souls . . . Each develops a Plan of Concentration that culminates in a senior project . . . The college is run in the style of a New England town meeting . . . Students have veto power over faculty hiring . . . Unable to lure minorities.

New School for Social Research (Eugene Lang College). Smack in the middle of Greenwich Village, Lang is the ultimate in bohemian funkiness . . . Offers little sense of community and virtually no campus life—New York City is Lang's campus . . . Tiny enrollment of 250, but access to a world-class university.

State University of New York/Purchase. Small state university (3,700) that specializes in the arts . . . Wooded Westchester campus is a hop and a skip from New York City . . . Greenwich Village is a frequent destination on the weekends . . . Large gay community.

Pitzer College. Like Hampshire, part of a prestigious five-college group (the Claremonts) . . . Also founded in the 1960s, with an emphasis on social and behavioral sciences . . . Offers a more traditional academic program than most other colleges on this list . . . Location east of L.A. is ideal except for smog.

Sarah Lawrence College. Favored outpost of the New York City–esque avant garde . . . Located in affluent Bronxville, half an hour from the city . . . Coed for several decades, but still overwhelmingly female . . . Students design their own curriculums with the help of a faculty don . . . Best known for writing and the arts.

☞See Also

College of the Atlantic (The Most Innovative Curriculums)
Beloit College (Other Excellent Small Colleges)
The Evergreen State College (Small-College Bargains)
Grinnell College (Top Colleges, Better Odds)
Lewis and Clark College (Other Excellent Small Colleges)
Oberlin College (Top Colleges, Better Odds)
Reed College (Top Colleges, Better Odds)

THE MOST INNOVATIVE CURRICULUMS

As a group, the following colleges are much more diverse than those in the previous group. The unorthodox colleges listed above are, first and foremost, magnets for unconventional students who want to be part of an unconventional community. Though many of those colleges also offer innovative curriculums, what defines the tenor of daily life has more to do with the kind of student they attract than what goes on inside the classroom.

The following list, on the other hand, includes colleges that are doing interesting things with curriculum that may appeal to a wide spectrum of students. Some of these colleges attract mainly traditionalists, and others attract mainly liberals, but the majority assemble students united only by their willingness to try something a little different. If that includes you, read on.

Alverno College. Small Wisconsin women's college that has pioneered competency-based education . . . Instead of letter grades, students receive "validations" in practical areas like communication, problem solving, and citizenship . . . Student body overwhelmingly from Wisconsin . . . Roman Catholic–affiliated.

College of the Atlantic. Oceanfront college in Bar Harbor, Maine, where everyone graduates with a degree in "human ecology" . . . Dedicated to the study of humankind's relationship to the environment . . . Still has trappings of its founding in the late 1960s as an alternative school . . . Tiny enrollment of about 200 students.

Bradford College. Tiny Massachusetts liberal arts college (500) that combines the liberal arts with career training . . . Curriculum emphasizes writing and majors that cut across the lines of traditional disciplines . . . Minors include marketing, management, and other practical fields . . . No SATs required, and admission is not difficult.

Brooklyn College. Has an innovative core curriculum that occupies students throughout freshman and sophomore years . . . Includes a comprehensive overview of Western culture and non-Western cultures . . . The college is a branch of the City University system . . . Most students are native Brooklynites.

Cornell College. Along with Colorado College, one of two schools in the nation where students study one course at a time . . . Not to be confused with the "other" Cornell of the Ivy League . . . Small-town Iowa location makes Cornell the less selective of the two . . . With 1,100 students, Cornell is half the size of other "small" schools . . . No classes with more than twenty-five students.

Deep Springs College. Picture 25 Ivy-caliber men alone in the desert for two years—that's Deep Springs College . . . Set on 50,000 acres at the arid border of Nevada and California . . . "Campus" consists of a few ranch-style buildings . . . Quirky, intellectual students transfer to top colleges after two years to finish undergraduate degrees.

Kalamazoo College. Small Michigan college specializing in off-campus internships and study abroad . . . Students spend sophomore through senior year alternating study with work in prospective career field(s) . . . K Plan culminates in a senior project that integrates both.

☞See Also

Top Nonconformist Colleges
Colorado College (Other Excellent Small Colleges)
St. John's College (Other Excellent Small Colleges)

ENVIRONMENTAL STUDIES AND INTERNATIONAL STUDIES: THE HOT INTERDISCIPLINARY MAJORS OF THE 1990S

It's a safe bet that all the colleges on any of our lists are going to have an English or history department. Not all, however, will offer majors in environmental studies or international studies. Though a student at any school can stitch together a concentration in one or the other, we thought it would be useful to list some of the best colleges that have particularly strong programs. Keep in mind that both lists include a wide assortment of colleges that may have absolutely nothing else in common. In the liberal arts, the personality match between school and student should remain paramount.

Environmental Studies
Allegheny College
College of the Atlantic
Bowdoin College
University of California/Davis
University of California/Santa Barbara
Colby College
University of Colorado/Boulder
Dartmouth College
Deep Springs College
Middlebury College

University of New Hampshire
University of North Carolina/Greensboro
Oberlin College
St. Lawrence University
Tulane University
University of Vermont
University of Washington

International Studies

American University
Austin College
Claremont McKenna College
Colby College
Connecticut College
Dartmouth College
Dickinson College
Georgetown University
George Washington University
Goucher College
Hiram College
Johns Hopkins University
Kalamazoo College
Lewis and Clark College
University of Massachusetts/Amherst
Middlebury College
Occidental College
Princeton University
Reed College
St. Olaf College
Sweet Briar College
College of William and Mary

STUDY-ABROAD PROGRAMS

We would also like to offer a word about study abroad. If that is one of your interests, the above international studies list is a good place to look. Virtually all those colleges also have strong study-abroad programs.

In general, the best study-abroad programs are offered by small liberal arts colleges. The Ivy League universities, except for Dartmouth, have always been lukewarm to the concept. (Princeton makes the list above because of its famed Woodrow Wilson School of Public and International Affairs.) A much higher percentage of students at the top liberal arts colleges spend a semester or year abroad.

If someone pulled out a gun and said, "Name the top five colleges in the nation for study abroad," we would probably list: Colby, Connecticut College, Dickinson, Kalamazoo, Lewis and Clark College, Middlebury, Occidental, and St. Olaf. (That's eight, but who's counting?)

COLLEGES FOR STUDENTS WITH LEARNING DISABILITIES

Accommodation for students with learning disabilities is among the fastest-growing—and most controversial—academic areas in higher education. A generation ago, few colleges paid much attention to LD students. But that has changed in the 1990s, with the sudden "discovery" that a significant segment of the population may suffer problems that qualify as learning disabilities. Services have multiplied on virtually all campuses. But so too has skepticism as to whether some of the newly diagnosed disorders really exist.

No one denies that some students do suffer from learning disabilities. The diagnosis must be made a by certified professional—usually a physician, psychologist, or learning specialist. Students are judged to be LD if their performance on particular types of tasks shows a pattern of being lower than their intelligence would suggest. These students suffer impaired performance not because of an inability to comprehend but because of breakdowns in their ability to perceive and process information.

A learning disability should not be confused with low achievement. Every student has strengths and weaknesses. Some work harder than others and do better as a result. But recently, some families have begun to press for LD classification with questionable evidence. Why? With increasing competition for good grades and admission to college, an LD diagnosis is an easy way to explain mediocre grades. More to the point, certified LD status allows students extra time on the PSAT and SAT. In the past ten years, applications to the Educational Testing Service for extra time have almost doubled, with most of the requests coming from affluent families who know how to use the system to their benefit.

Meanwhile, some colleges have begun to wonder whether the LD movement has gone too far. Boston University, an erstwhile leader in LD services, recently made sharp cuts in its program. Many colleges have become more skeptical of LD classification when the initial diagnosis is made on the eve of the college search.

Despite the doubts, students with legitimate disabilities will find high-quality services at many colleges. Virtually all major institutions, from Harvard to the local community college, provide support for the learning disabled. Assistance may include printed notes of lectures, tapes, or extended time on exams. Our first list includes major universities offering particularly strong services; the smaller schools in the second list all devote major emphasis to LD students.

Our advice for LD students? Check out the support services yourself at each college on your list. If possible, pay a visit to the LD support office or have a phone conversation with one of the administrators. Since many such programs depend on the expertise of one or two people, the quality of the services can change abruptly with changes in staff.

Major Universities with Strong Support for Students with Learning Disabilities

Adelphi University
American University
University of Arizona
University of California/Berkeley
Clark University
University of Colorado/Boulder
University of Denver
DePaul University
University of Georgia
Hofstra University
Purdue University
Rochester Institute of Technology
Syracuse University
University of Vermont
University of Virginia

Small Colleges with Strong Support Services for Learning Disabled Students

Bard College
Bradford College
Curry College
Landmark College
Loras College
Lynn University
Marist College
Mercyhurst College

Mitchell College
Muskingum College
University of New England
St. Thomas Aquinas College
Southern Vermont College
Westminster College (Missouri)
West Virginia Wesleyan College

For Pre-Professionals Only: A Subject-by-Subject Guide

Though liberal arts education is the best springboard to most careers, there are a few professions that require specialized training. If medicine is your goal, a standard list of science courses found in most liberal arts colleges will be all you need at the undergraduate level. But if you want to be an engineer, it takes more than just a strong background in science. You need highly technical preparation in a structured sequence, the kind of preparation that you simply can't get outside of a college of engineering. If you like music, you can dabble in performance at a liberal arts college and maybe even do a major. But if your life's dream is to be a headliner at Carnegie Hall, you'll probably need to prepare at a conservatory, where people give their heart and soul to music. Likewise, you can do a studio art major at most colleges and universities. But if you're the type who never does a lick of academic homework yet stays up until 3:00 A.M. doing art assignments, that's a clue that maybe you should be ticketed for art school.

Below, we offer lists of prominent schools in seven academic areas where students may choose specialized undergraduate training: engineering, architecture, business, art/design, the performing arts, communications/journalism, and film/television. If you are planning a career in one or another of these areas, your college search will consist largely of finding the best program for you in that particular area. In contrast to the liberal arts section, we list only names here. It is your job to assess the strengths and weaknesses of each program, according to your needs. You may notice, however, that some of the schools mentioned here for specialized training are also described in one or another of the liberal arts categories. We encourage you to consult *The Fiske Guide to Colleges* for a full write-up on most institutions listed in this section. If you cannot find them there, consult the recommended-reading chapter for other publications that will include descriptions.

We also recommend that you shop for a school that will give you an adequate dose of liberal arts. For that matter, you might consider a double major (or minor) in a liberal arts field to complement your area of technical expertise. If you allow yourself to get too specialized too soon, you may end up as tomorrow's equivalent of the typewriter repairman. In a rapidly changing job market, nothing is so practical as the ability to read, write, and think.

ENGINEERING

Were you the kind of kid who always made a beeline for the blocks in nursery school? Or spent years trying to blow up the family garage with your chemistry set? Are you the kind of person who gets a kick out of staring into a computer screen for hours to solve an obscure problem? Is your idea of a good time to curl up with a description of Albert Einstein's Theory of Relativity?

If some or all of the above apply, you could be ticketed for a career in engineering, a field that combines chemistry, physics, math, and computer science for building and design. Getting the degree, however, is easier said than done. Would-be engineers must persevere through a highly structured curriculum that includes heavy doses of higher math and science (and often takes five years to complete). If that doesn't sound like your cup of tea, it probably isn't. The pathway to an engineering degree is littered with students who went into it for the wrong reasons, such as "My dad wanted me to be an engineer" or "I wanted a job." The only good reason to be an engineer is that you enjoy the work. Otherwise, you'll soon find out why they call it "pre-business" at many universities.

Don't assume that potential employers will be beating down your door, either. Some engineering majors offer excellent job prospects; others have fallen on hard times. Aerospace engineering has been the latest to crash and burn, because of sweeping cutbacks at NASA.

Play the Field

If you think engineering is for you, there are a number of different routes you can take. The purest dose of engineering education is found at technical institutes and universities that specialize in engineering. Nothing in the world of technology can match the intensity of thousands of bright minds living and breathing computers and engineering. The downside of these sorts of places comes from the very thing that makes them great: they tend to be one-dimensional. A technical community without English majors or artists tends to take on a slightly bizarre, ingrown quality. Technical institutes are also overwhelmingly male, and the skewed sex ratio doesn't help social life.

If a technical institute seems a bit hard-core, there are several other options. Most top students choose to study at a large private university that has a college of engineering. These universities have a critical mass of engineers but also offer a broad spectrum of courses in the arts and sciences, business, and numerous other fields. Cost-conscious students often opt for a variation on this theme: the large public university. In effect, these students trade a little prestige for an education that is easier on the wallet. The major drawback of both these types of institutions, and many technical institutes as well, is that they are so darn big. As in every other field, the lowly undergrad engineers can get stuck playing second fiddle to the graduate students—or worse, taking their courses from the graduate students.

This leads us to a fourth type of engineering school, the small college or university. As you know by now, small is beautiful in education, because students get more attention from faculty and more chance for involvement. At many of these institutions, undergraduates are able to perform the kind of research that only graduate students are allowed to do at big universities. Engineering education also tends to be more firmly rooted in the liberal arts at the smaller schools. Often, though not always, engineering students at these colleges complete much of the same liberal arts core as every other student. The questions to ask at these schools include: Do they have a critical mass of engineers? Do they have facilities that stack up well with the larger universities? Do they have the same access to engineering employers? If the answer to these questions is yes, you may have found the best place to get an engineering degree.

A final way to get an engineering degree is to enroll in a 3–2 program. The numbers refer to the years spent at each of two schools. For the first three, a student enrolls in a small liberal arts college and takes a variety of pre-engineering courses, as well as a full helping of the humanities and social sciences. For the last two years, the student transfers to a university with an engineering program to complete the technical education. The program is a year longer (and a year more expensive), but the student finishes with two degrees—one in engineering and one in the liberal arts. Most of the top liberal arts colleges in the nation offer 3–2 programs, and many come with virtually guaranteed admission to the engineering programs at prestigious universities such as Columbia or Washington U. in St. Louis.

Top Technical Institutes

California Institute of Technology (Caltech)
Colorado School of Mines*
Cooper Union for the Advancement of Science and Art
Florida Institute of Technology
Georgia Institute of Technology (Georgia Tech)*
Harvey Mudd College
Illinois Institute of Technology
Massachusetts Institute of Technology
New Mexico Institute of Mining and Technology*
Rensselaer Polytechnic Institute
Rochester Institute of Technology
Rose-Hulman Institute of Technology
Stevens Institute of Technology
Worcester Polytechnic Institute

Private Universities Strong in Engineering

Carnegie Mellon University
Case Western Reserve University
Cornell University
Duke University
Johns Hopkins University
Northwestern University
University of Notre Dame
University of Pennsylvania
Stanford University
Tufts University
Tulane University
Vanderbilt University
Washington University (Missouri)

Public Universities Strong in Engineering

University of California/Berkeley
University of California/Los Angeles
Clemson University
University of Illinois/Urbana-Champaign
Iowa State University
University of Michigan
Michigan State University
State University of New York/Buffalo

*Public institutions.

Pennsylvania State University
Purdue University
Rutgers University
Texas A&M University
Virginia Polytechnic Institute and State University (Virginia Tech)
University of Washington

Small Colleges and Universities Strong in Engineering
Brown University
Bucknell University
Calvin College
Clarkson University
Dartmouth College
Lafayette College
Lehigh University
University of the Pacific
University of Redlands
Rice University
Swarthmore College
Trinity College (Connecticut)
Tuskegee University
Union College

ARCHITECTURE

Learning to be an architect consists of two basic elements that don't always go together. A student must learn (1) the physics and structural fundamentals of building, and (2) the aesthetics of building and how architectural structures meet human needs. A good architect combines the eye for physics of the engineer with the humanistic sensibility of the artist. Unfortunately, engineers and artists mix like oil and water, and it is rare to find either a student or an architecture program that offers a perfect combination of the two. Most architecture programs look very much like engineering schools, but some have an artsy streak that gives them more of an alternative flavor (purple hair is always a good tip-off). Before you choose an architecture program, think about what sort of architecture "personality" best fits your needs.

Most aspiring architects get their training in a conventional college or school of architecture. The students at these schools may not design the prettiest buildings, but at least you know the buildings won't fall down. A smaller number of architecture programs exist within a more liberal arts context, sometimes in a department of architecture within a college of arts and sciences. Usually, though not always, these programs place more emphasis on aesthetics. When looking at an architecture program, check out its ties to the engineering and/or the art program. That will provide an important clue as to where it stands.

The size of the program is a consideration, as well as the ratio of graduate students to undergrads. See if there will be any opportunities to work with the graduate students, as opposed to merely being taught by them. As in engineering, students may also opt for a 3–2 program—three years at a liberal arts college doing "pre-architecture" and the liberal arts, followed by two years in an architecture program to complete the professional training. Though 3–2 takes five years, the end product is a broader education and degrees in both a liberal arts field and architecture.

Unfortunately, the job market is a major concern for anyone contemplating architecture. The commercial building glut of the 1990s has made for some lean times in recent years, and no one can say for sure how many jobs there will be in 2005 or 2010.

Private Universities Strong in Architecture

Carnegie Mellon University
Columbia University
Cooper Union for the Advancement of Science and Art
Cornell University
Howard University
Lehigh University
Massachusetts Institute of Technology
University of Notre Dame
Princeton University
Rensselaer Polytechnic Institute
Rice University
Tulane University
Washington University (Missouri)

Public Universities Strong in Architecture

University of California/Berkeley
University of Cincinnati
Georgia Institute of Technology (George Tech)
University of Illinois/Urbana-Champaign
University of Kansas
Miami University (Ohio)

University of Michigan
State University of New York/Buffalo
University of Oregon
Pennsylvania State University
University of Texas/Austin
Virginia Polytechnic Institute and State University (Virginia Tech)
University of Washington

A Few Arts-Oriented Architecture Programs

Barnard College
Bennington College
Pratt Institute
Rhode Island School of Design
Wellesley College
Yale University

BUSINESS

Preparation for a career in "business" is a much-misunderstood subject. There are approximately 150 million adults in the United States, and most of them are in business of some sort. Everything from aardvark farming to zeppelin repair falls under the heading of business. Yet a myth persists that the only path to enter the business world is through an undergraduate business major. In fact, many people major in something else and find that experience is the best teacher when it comes to business skills. Others wait until graduate school to get their business training.

If you want to climb the corporate ladder, you shouldn't necessarily go off to business school right away and hit the library every night with *Principles of Accounting*. Consider the example of Michael Eisner, Chairman and CEO of the Walt Disney Corporation. Eisner went to Denison University, a small institution that doesn't even have a business program, and majored in English literature and theater. With no other degrees, he rose to become one of the most powerful executives in the entertainment industry. (The biggest titan of the business world, Bill Gates, is a college dropout— albeit from Harvard.)

There are advantages and disadvantages to majoring in business at the undergraduate level. In the short run, graduates are probably better positioned for entry-level jobs in accounting, marketing, banking, and similar fields. When the job market is tight, that can be a real plus. Unfortunately, an undergraduate business major can also be a limiting factor. Most top graduate programs prefer applicants who have majored in something else, preferably the liberal arts. These schools want applicants who got a broad education and learned to think; they supply the business training. (Most of the top business schools don't even offer undergraduate programs.) Among mid- and top-level managers, very few will have made it to their positions with only an undergraduate business major. The accounting major who feels so smug about his job prospects now may someday find himself taking orders from a hopelessly impractical art history major who went back five years later for an M.B.A.

If you do want business training at the undergraduate level, there are two primary choices: a college of business, or an economics major in a college of arts and sciences. The college of business will offer a full range of majors in all the primary business areas, including specialties like international business and management information systems. The business training is likely to be specialized and extensive, but it may come at the cost of a firm grounding in the liberal arts.

An economics major can be had at just about any liberal arts college or university. The treatment of business-related topics is likely to be more theoretical than practical, but included in the deal will be a liberal arts degree.

Private Universities Strong in Business

Carnegie Mellon University
Case Western Reserve University
Emory University
Georgetown University
Howard University
Massachusetts Institute of Technology
New York University
University of Notre Dame
University of Pennsylvania
Rensselaer Polytechnic Institute
University of Richmond
Tulane University
Wake Forest University
Washington University (Missouri)

Public Universities Strong in Business

University of California/Berkeley
University of Florida
University of Illinois/Urbana-Champaign
Indiana University
Miami University (Ohio)
University of Michigan
State University of New York/Albany
University of North Carolina/Chapel Hill
University of Vermont
University of Virginia
College of William and Mary

Small Colleges and Universities Strong in Business

Babson College
Bucknell University
Claremont McKenna College
DePauw University
Fairfield University
Franklin and Marshall College
Gettysburg College
Hendrix College
Lehigh University
Lewis and Clark College
Morehouse College
Ohio Wesleyan University
Skidmore College
Trinity University (Texas)
Washington and Lee University

ART AND DESIGN

These days, an art major sounds like something out of a TV sitcom. Picture yourself having a heart-to-heart with dear old Dad—the person who is financing your education to the tune of $100,000—and gently breaking the news.

"Dad, I've decided to be an art major."

When Dad regains consciousness, he'll probably have visions of you selling apples on a street corner or living out of a 1960s Volkswagon van.

In reality, Dad is only half right. Making a living as a painter or a sculptor ranges somewhere between difficult and impossible. But an education in art and design is more than just painting pretty pictures. There are plenty of jobs in advertising, publishing, fashion design, illustration, interior decoration, arts management, and a host of other fields for students who can apply artistic skills to practical careers. Some of today's most interesting work in art and design takes place on that most practical of modern canvases, the computer. Hollywood is desperate to find computer-savvy animators.

If you are looking to pursue an art-related career, a number of choices await. The most important question may well be whether you want to study in a specialized art school or pursue an art major in a liberal arts college or university. Each has its merits. The specialized schools offer unmatched intensity of collective soul searching that only a community of artists can generate. The caliber of work is likely to be extremely high, and the pathways to careers in art and design are likely to be well-worn. Students will also get the benefit of extensive alumni networks and instant school-name recognition from those in the field.

As a side note, the nomenclature in art and design can get pretty confusing. Some institutions call themselves schools or colleges of "art" or "visual arts," others use "design," and still others say "art and design." In the art world, the term "design" has a more pre-professional ring to it, while "art" signifies a purer form of expression. That distinction doesn't always mean anything when it comes to the names of particular institutions, many of which were acquired decades or even centuries ago. But the difference is significant in your choice of major. At some schools, the art and design departments work closely; at others, the two are worlds apart.

The main drawbacks of an art school are the lack of broad liberal arts training and the inability to major in non-art fields. These schools are probably not the best choice if you have any doubts about your commitment to art, or if you would like to combine art or design with another major. Most good colleges and universities have departments of studio art and graphic design, and many of them offer superior training as well as chances for cross-disciplinary work in seemingly unrelated fields. The atmosphere is likely to be less single-minded and more relaxed, though a high-powered art department can generate plenty of intensity with a core of committed students.

Top Schools of Art and Design

Art Center College of Design (California)
California Institute of the Arts
Cooper Union of the Advancement of Science and Art
Maryland Institute, College of Art
Massachusetts College of Art

Moore College of Art and Design
North Carolina School of the Arts
Otis Institute of Art and Design
Parsons School of Design
Pratt Institute
Rhode Island School of Design
School of the Art Institute of Chicago
School of Visual Arts

Major Universities Strong in Art and Design

Boston University
Carnegie Mellon University
University of Cincinnati
Cornell University
Harvard University
University of Michigan
New York University
University of Pennsylvania
University of Rochester
Washington University (Missouri)
University of Washington

Small Colleges and Universities Strong in Art and Design

Alfred University
Bard College
Bradford College
Brown University
Furman University
Hollins College
Kenyon College
Lake Forest College
Manhattanville College
State University of New York/Purchase
Randolph-Macon Woman's College
University of North Carolina/Greensboro
Skidmore College
Smith College
Williams College

THE PERFORMING ARTS

The story line on the performing arts is similar to the one for art and design. Earning a living on stage is even harder than in the studio, and performing skills lead to fewer related professions. Aside from teaching and arts management, there is not much a would-be performer can do besides playing or singing. (Even areas such as production and set design are tough to crack.) A performing-arts major as part of a liberal arts education can be perfectly fine for pre-law, pre-med—pre–almost anything. But students in this category should probably pay at least as much attention to the overall match as they do to the quality of the arts programs.

If music is your passion, you have a choice similar to that of the artists. You can either study in a conservatory dedicated entirely to music, or you can pick a liberal arts college or university with a strong music program. The conservatory route is legendary for the intense pressure to perform—literally—but it probably offers the best shot for a career as a musician. If you're not ready to give heart and soul (and possibly sanity) to music, you're probably better off attending a comprehensive institution with a strong music program.

The same applies to future actors and dancers. In most cases, a good drama or dance program at a college or university will provide ample opportunities. For "Broadway or Bust" types, a handful of the arts specialty schools offer high-powered training. The legendary Juilliard School in New York maintains world-class programs in all the major performing arts. A few others, notably North Carolina School of the Arts and California Institute of the Arts, cover the entire spectrum of art, design, music, dance, and drama.

If you are considering a particular conservatory or arts school, pay close attention to its specialities. Music schools are strong in different instruments; dance schools emphasize different types of performing. Creative philosophies at arts schools vary widely, and much will hinge on your working relationship with the mentors of the program in your area. Lastly, we recommend that specialty-school shoppers keep an eye out for ties to nearby colleges. Since most arts schools are located in a city, they often have cross-registration with major universities. To the performing artist, few things are more important than a broad exposure to the liberal arts.

Top Music Conservatories

Berklee College of Music
Boston Conservatory
California Institute of the Arts
Cleveland Institute of Music

Curtis Institute of Music
Eastman School of Music
Juilliard School
Manhattan School of Music
New England Conservatory of Music
North Carolina School of the Arts
Peabody Conservatory of Music
San Francisco Conservatory of Music

Major Universities Strong in Music

Boston University
University of California/Los Angeles
Carnegie Mellon University
Case Western Reserve University
University of Colorado/Boulder
Harvard University
Indiana University
Ithaca College
University of Miami (Florida)
University of Michigan
University of Nebraska/Lincoln
New York University
Northwestern University
Rice University
University of Southern California
Yale University

Small Colleges and Universities Strong in Music

Bard College
Bennington College
Butler University
DePauw University
Illinois Wesleyan University
Lawrence University*
Loyola University (Illinois)
Manhattanville College
Mills College
Oberlin College*
St. Olaf College

*These two are unique because they combine a world-class conservatory with a top-notch liberal arts college.

Sarah Lawrence College
Skidmore College
Smith College
Wesleyan University
Wheaton College (Illinois)

Major Universities Strong in Drama

Boston College
Boston University
University of California/Los Angeles
Carnegie Mellon University
The Catholic University of America
DePaul University
Fordham University
Indiana University
Ithaca College
New York University
Northwestern University
University of North Carolina/Chapel Hill
University of Southern California
Southern Methodist University
Syracuse University
University of Washington
Yale University

Small Colleges and Universities Strong in Drama

Bennington College
Bradford College
Connecticut College
Juilliard School
Kenyon College
Lawrence University
Macalester College
State University of New York/Purchase
Otterbein College
Princeton University
Rollins College
Sarah Lawrence College
Skidmore College
Vassar College

Major Universities Strong in Dance

Arizona State University
University of California/Irvine
University of California/Los Angeles
Case Western Reserve University
Florida State University
Indiana University
New York University
State University of New York/Purchase
Ohio University
Southern Methodist University
University of Texas/Austin
Washington University (Missouri)

Small Colleges and Universities Strong in Dance

Amherst College
Barnard College
Bennington College
Butler University
Connecticut College
Dartmouth College
Goucher College
Juilliard School
Kenyon College
North Carolina School of the Arts
Princeton University
Sarah Lawrence College
Smith College
State University of New York/Purchase

COMMUNICATIONS/JOURNALISM

Though the pundits constantly tell us that we live in the Information Age, they could just as easily call it the Communications Age. Demand for graduates with media and other communications skills has soared in the past several decades, and so too has the number of programs to train them. For students who want an education in communications, there are two ways to get it: (1) attend an excellent college or university and major in a liberal arts field; (2) enroll in a college of communications for pre-professional training in a particular field. Among the latter, journalism is usually the most eye-catching for high school students. (Though a few universities offer a full-fledged school of journalism, the subject is usually offered as a department within communications.) Other important communications fields include advertising, public relations, speech, and broadcasting. (Students interested in broadcasting should also read the section on film/television that follows.)

Before enrolling in a college of communications, keep in mind that many of the skills important for success are the same ones you learn in a liberal arts program. Writing is the heart of advertising, journalism, and public relations. Corporations won't mind teaching a good writer about the particulars of advertising; few will waste time with a graduate who knows about advertising but can't write. The same applies to journalism. Many journalism programs offer fine preparation, but so too do many liberal arts institutions, where a good campus newspaper often provides more than enough hands-on experience. For budding journalists, a liberal arts education is virtually a trade school course of study—one that teaches disciplinal curiosity, research skills, communication skills, and a sense of perspective. The best undergraduate journalism programs understand this and build in heavy doses of liberal arts. Beware of any that does not.

For students interested in broadcasting—especially TV—the case for pre-professional training is a bit stronger, largely because of the expensive facilities required for a topflight program. Students considering broadcast journalism should remember that unless you are physically attractive, your chances of ending up in front of the camera are virtually nil.

No matter what route they choose, students interested in communications or journalism should seek broad exposure to many fields. Those who specialize too soon may find that they have nothing interesting to say.

As the following list illustrates, communications/journalism programs are confined mainly to state universities and a smattering of private ones. Most of the nation's elite colleges have a program of their own for budding journalists: the English department.

Major Universities Strong in Communications/Journalism

American University
Boston University
University of California/Los Angeles
University of Florida
University of Georgia
University of Illinois/Urbana-Champaign
Indiana University
University of Michigan

University of Missouri/Columbia
University of North Carolina/Chapel Hill
Northwestern University
Ohio University
University of Southern California
Stanford University
Syracuse University

FILM/TELEVISION

When it comes to glamour, few professions can match the film and television industry. But if you're among the cast of thousands who dream of making it big in Hollywood, be prepared to hustle. Getting a toehold in film or broadcasting is no easy task, and making it big is even harder.

There is no primrose path to a career in film or broadcasting. As a seventeen- or eighteen-year-old high school graduate, your best bet is to get a well-rounded education. The liberal arts are especially crucial if you are interested in the creative elements of film production. The technical stuff can be learned anytime, but no film course can teach you imagination, creativity, how to write, or how to tell a story. Many film-industry insiders advise students to wait until the graduate level for specialized film training. A good liberal arts college with a critical mass of people interested in film is often the best preparation.

The main advantage of undergraduate film school is the chance to rub shoulders with other aspiring actors, writers, directors, producers, and cinematographers. If intense competition and single-minded focus bring out your best, film school is definitely worth considering. Some programs are part of a college of communications or journalism; others are linked to theater arts. A "school" or "college" of broadcasting or film and TV is often (though not always) more comprehensive than a "department" of film. Among major university film schools, three stand out: University of Southern California's School of Cinema-Television (George Lucas, Ron Howard); UCLA's School of Theater, Film, and Television (Francis Ford Coppola, Tim Robbins); and New York University's Film and Television Department (Billy Crystal, Spike Lee, Martin Scorsese, Oliver Stone). More unusual is tiny Columbia College in Hollywood, one of the few undergraduate colleges in the nation devoted entirely to media arts.

Making your mark in the film industry takes talent, hard work, and a high tolerance for rejection. Though the dream of being the next Steven Spielberg dies hard, a more realistic approach is to consider the many opportunities outside the world of big-budget feature films. As long as the role of media in our society continues to expand, so too will opportunities in broadcast- and film-related professions.

Major Universities Strong in Film/Television

Arizona State University
Boston University
University of California/Los Angeles
University of Cincinnati
University of Florida
University of Kansas
Memphis State University
University of Michigan
New York University
Northwestern University
Pennsylvania State University
University of Southern California
Syracuse University
University of Texas/Austin
Wayne State University

Small Colleges and Universities Strong in Film/Television

Bard College
Beloit College
Brown University
California Institute of the Arts
Columbia College (California)
Hampshire College
Hofstra University
Ithaca College
State University of New York/Purchase
Occidental College
Pitzer College
Pomona College
Sarah Lawrence College
School of Visual Arts

7
Where to Learn More

When your parents were in high school, there was no great mystery about where to find information about colleges. The choice was between a few old stand-bys like *Lovejoy's* and *Peterson's* that offered a column or two of statistics on each school.

But those were also the days when most people still ate corn flakes or Rice Krispies for breakfast and got all their television from the three major networks. Today, breakfast cereals take up a whole aisle in the grocery store and most people aren't satisfied with 30 channels of cable TV. The college-guide shelf of the late nineties is crowded with entries written from every conceivable angle, and the rise of the Internet has created a whole new universe of information. The problem: how to sort through it all. You can either hire your own reference librarian or read through the overview that follows on the best sources for each step in the process.

INFORMATION ABOUT COLLEGES

The key is to understand the two steps of the process: (1) generating a list of colleges, and (2) getting the inside story on them. As noted in "Getting a Jump Start," computer resources are handy for generating names based on various criteria (size, location, majors, etc.), but they rarely offer detailed descriptions. Until authors of printed guides figure out how to make money on the Internet, their online sites will offer only enough information to encourage book purchases.

Before buying any information source—especially software or CD-ROMs—find out if it is also available in your guidance office. You may find some of what you need there.

Below are our picks for the best college resources listed within each category in order (more or less) of their usefulness to a majority of students.

SOURCES FOR BUILDING A LIST OF COLLEGES

The College Finder, by Steven Antonoff. Ballantine Books. Features lists of recommended colleges in hundreds of categories, ranging from colleges with the most National Merit Scholars to colleges that operate kosher kitchens.

America's Best Colleges, U.S. News & World Report. If you've learned the concept of insignificant figures in science class, you've taken the first step toward understanding the *U.S. News* rankings. No one in education takes these numbers seriously (except to use for public relations), because the formula tries to quantify what are essentially qualitative judgments and because the rankings magnify trivial differences. But the lists can be useful for generating new prospects at the beginning stages of a search. The regional lists are an especially good place to find outstanding colleges that may not be household names. Check the Web (http://www.usnews.com) for the rankings and other college entrance material.

Index of Majors and Graduate Degrees, The College Board. The counselor's Bible listing all of the colleges that offer every conceivable major from accounting to zoology.

The National College Databank, Peterson's Guides. Another book full of lists of colleges. Especially useful for its section on the colleges that offer various varsity sports.

A profusion of World Wide Web sites are also built around college search programs packaged with admissions advice, financial aid info, chat rooms, etc. Below we give you a baker's dozen of the most prominent ones. Surf them all if you like, but think twice before agreeing to buy anything.

College Assist	http://www.edworks.com/index.htm
College Board On-line	http://www.collegeboard.org
College Counsel	http://www.ccounsel.com
The College Guide	http://www.jayi.com/ACG
College Edge	http://www.collegeedge.com

College Net	http://www.collegenet.com
College Scape	http://www.collegescape.com
College Town	http://www.ctown.com
College Select	http://www.CollegeSelect.com
College View	http://www.collegeview.com
Internet College Exchange	http://www.usmall.com
Peterson's	http://www.petersons.com
The Princeton Review	http://www.review.com

COLLEGE GUIDES AND RELATED WEB SITES

The Fiske Guide to Colleges, by Edward B. Fiske. Times Books. Includes critical essays on approximately 300 of the best and most interesting colleges in the nation. The best place to begin the college search for applicants to selective colleges.

Student Advantage Guide to the Best 310 Colleges, The Princeton Review Publishing Company. Covers a selection of colleges similar to that of the *Fiske Guide.* Useful for comparisons, though you should ignore the dubious What's Hot/What's Not section. Excerpts from this book are also available at the *Review*'s Web site.

The Insider's Guide to the Colleges, Yale Daily News. St. Martin's Press. A guide to selective colleges, produced by students at Yale. Another counterpoint to the *Fiske Guide.*

The College Catalogue, Kaplan Educational Centers and Simon & Schuster. Includes 1,000 schools nationwide with more detail on several hundred of the most selective.

College Choice & Admissions (http://www.collegeguides.com) The best overview of all sources for college and financial aid information (besides this one). Its ratings of the college guides and Web sites are right on target. The same people publish a book called *The Best Resources for College Choice & Admission* (Resource Pathways, Inc.).

Colleges That Change Lives, by Loren Pope. Penguin Books. Long profiles of forty small colleges "that you should know about even if you're not a straight-A student." Makes the case that these schools prepare students better than the Ivy League.

Yahoo Education Directory (http://www.yahoo.com) One of many directories of college Web pages (any other will do). Simply click on education, universities, and United States for an alphabetical listing. Keep in mind Web pages are produced by administrators trying to polish their school's image. Our advice: check out the sites under student organizations (especially newspapers). That's where you'll get the real story.

Peterson's Competitive Colleges, Peterson's Guides. The best statistical guide to the selective colleges. Offers one-page profiles of 375 schools.

Cass and Birnbaum's Guide to American Colleges, by Melissa Cass and Julia Cass Liepmann. HarperCollins Publishers. A comprehensive guide that mixes statistics and prose descriptions. Good for applicants to moderately selective and nonselective colleges.

Student Net (http://www.student.net/home.html) This site includes a directory of the home pages of students from over 250 colleges. Click on the school of your choice and browse through dozens or hundreds of students. When you find someone who shares your interests, e-mail a question or two about the school. Most people will respond.

SPECIAL-INTEREST GUIDES

Barron's Best Buys in College Education, by Lucia Solorzano. Barron's Educational Series. Profiles of 300 best buys for the college bargain hunter.

The College Board Guide to 150 Popular College Majors, College Entrance Examination Board. Articles on various majors written by experts in the field. An excellent resource for students who are undecided about what to study.

The Complete Guide to College Visits, by Janet Spencer and Sandra Maleson. Citadel Press. Provides nuts-and-bolts information on how to get there, where to stay, and travel time between colleges.

The Multicultural Student's Guide to Colleges, by Robert Mitchell. The Noonday Press. Articles on 200 selective colleges from a minority perspective. The best book of its type.

The Performing Arts Major's College Guide, by Carole J. Everett. Macmillan. Includes factual profiles and lists of the "most highly recommended programs" in various performing arts.

Professional Degree Programs in the Visual and Performing Arts, Peterson's Guides. Factual profiles of 900 programs.

The Complete Guide to American Film Schools, by Earnest Pintoff. Penguin Books. Provides largely statistical profiles of 600 programs in television and film, with a brief subjective assessment of each.

Education for the Earth: The College Guide for Careers in the Environment, Peterson's Guides. Factual profiles of 200 environment-related programs.

Making a Difference College Guide, by Miriam Weinstein. The Princeton Review. Profiles of over 100 "outstanding colleges to help you make a better world." Particular emphasis on environmental studies and community service.

Jewish Student's Guide to American Colleges, by Lee Goldberg. Sure Sellers. Subjective descriptions of Jewish life at approximately 100 colleges.

The K & W Guide to Colleges for the Learning Disabled, by Marybeth Kravets and Imy F. Wax. HarperCollins. Factual profiles of LD programs at 200 colleges, with ratings for "level of support."

FINANCIAL AID

The Financial Aid Information Page (http://www.finaid.org) A terrific site that covers every angle of the aid search with numerous links. Includes free access to FastWeb, one of the nation's best scholarship databases.

You Can Afford College, by Bart Astor. Kaplan Source Books. Detailed coverage of the financial-aid process through the eyes of fictitious students.

Don't Miss Out: The Ambitious Student's Guide to Financial Aid, by Anna Leider and Robert Leider. Octameron Associates. A concise little guide that summarizes the essentials of financial aid. The complete text of the book is available online at http://jerome.signet.com/collegemoney/tocl.html.

Peterson's College Money Handbook, Peterson's Guides. Descriptions of costs and scholarship opportunities at over 1,700 four-year schools.

Cash for College: The Ultimate Guide to College Scholarships, by Cynthia Ruiz McKee, and Phillip C. McKee, Jr. Hearst Books. Includes listings of thousands of scholarships, cross-referenced by category.

The Scholarship Book: The Complete Guide to Private Sector Scholarships, Grants, and Loans for Undergraduates, by Daniel J. Cassidy. Prentice Hall. A cross-referenced listing of more than a thousand scholarships.

TEST PREP

There are literally dozens of books and software programs on how to prepare for, beat, ace, and psych out the various standardized tests. They generally fall into one of two categories:

- The no-nonsense models, which include vocabulary lists, formula reviews, and practice tests.
- The more provocative variety that promises to teach you how to outthink the test maker.

The former kind is a safer bet, though if you find one with a system that works for you, there is no reason not to get one of the latter. We recommend that you go to the nearest bookstore and spend a few minutes browsing the various offerings. How many vocabulary words do the books have? How many practice tests? How much emphasis do they place on test-taking techniques versus learning the material? Look for substance as well as style.

Material on the SAT IIs and ACT is less than abundant than that for the SAT I, but still readily available at most large bookstores. The best place to begin is *The College Board's Official Guide to the SAT II: Subject Tests,* which includes sample problems from each. This book will be particularly valuable for students who haven't decided which SAT II tests to take and want to gauge their preparation in each subject. For more in-depth coverage, books devoted to a single SAT II test are also available.

The World Wide Web is home to a number of test-prep sites. We recommend surfing several before putting down any money. Some of them offer free "web-ware" that is a scaled down version of software available for purchase. The following is an alphabetical list of some of the best sites. The education directory of any Web search engine will give you more.

Chancellor and Dean	http://www.cdean.com
College PowerPrep	http://www.powerprep.com
Kaplan Educational Centers	http://www.kaplan.com
The Princeton Review	http://www.review.com
Prep Doctor.com	http://www.prepdoctor.com
SAT Dominator	http://www.loop.com/~costmo/
Stanford Testing Systems	http://www.testprep.com
Tesuji	http://www.tesuji.com

ELECTRONIC FORMS AND TEST REGISTRATION

Anything that can be filled out on paper is also available on your computer screen. In addition to the colleges with downloadable application forms on their Web sites, numerous private companies (including many of those listed under "Sources for Building a List of Colleges") offer hundreds of them that can be downloaded. Some of the latter offer the added bonus that personal information can be typed in once and then reproduced on every application. Below are two of the best-known firms that specialize in electronic applications, along with three sites from which you can order admissions and financial aid forms.

Apply! (http://www.weapply.com)   This site offers one of the best deals on the Web: a free CD-ROM that features application forms from more than 500 participating colleges. The disk comes via U.S. mail, so be sure to order at least six weeks before you plan to file your applications.

CollegeLink (http://www.collegelink.com)   This site includes forms from more than 800 colleges that are available for downloading. Simply fill them out and transmit electronically to CollegeLink. They'll send you a printed copy in the mail for proofing. Your first application is free; additional ones are $5 each.

U.S. Department of Education, Office of Postsecondary Education (http://www.ed.gov/offices/OPE/) The federal government's information hub for students seeking financial aid. The site allows students to download a copy of the Free Application for Federal Student Aid (FAFSA).

College Board On-line (http://www.collegeboard.org) Students can use this site to register for the Financial Aid Profile, a supplemental form required by many elite schools. Students can also register here for the SAT I and II.

National Association of Secondary School Principals (http://www.nassp.org) The useful part of this site is a downloadable copy of the Common Application, a form accepted by more than 250 selective colleges, from Harvard to Harvey Mudd.

PART TWO

GETTING IN

8
Inside the
Admissions Process

S ome signs of the times:

A parent calls the Harvard University admissions office asking for advice about the best nursery schools to prepare his toddler for admission. . . . A student at an elite prep school files twenty-five college applications, including one to every Ivy League school. . . . A parent spends $2,000 for a consultant to help her child fill out college applications and write essays.

Welcome to the brave new world of college admissions. Though getting into college has always been a preoccupation of high school seniors, the intensity and determination of the struggle have reached new heights. In the chapter that follows, we'll take you on a tour of how the highly selective admissions process works. The rest of the book offers some strategies for success.

But we begin this section with another sign of the times that is not as well publicized. While a few elite schools have been flooded with applications, most of the 2,200 four-year colleges in the nation are hustling to entice enough students to fill their classes. These include some that have strong national reputations and others you've probably never heard of. But many of both have superb academic offerings, as well as an excellent record of launching graduates into fulfilling careers. Before you contemplate the dog-eat-dog competition at the elite, remember that you have other options.

Selectivity of American Four-Year Colleges

Admit 10 to 49% of applicants	7%
Admit 50 to 74% of applicants	28%
Admit 75 to 99% of applicants	54%
Open admissions	10%

Source: College Board

MOST COLLEGES ACCEPT ALL QUALIFIED APPLICANTS

As we learned in Chapter 5, "Cutting Through the Propaganda," colleges often pose as being more selective than they are. Most are still recovering from the "birth dearth," a plunge of almost one-third in the number of high school graduates from the late 1970s to the early 1990s.

Just look at the numbers. A generous definition of "selective" would be a college that turns away as many applicants as it accepts. According to estimates by the College Board, no more than 7 percent of four-year colleges in the country—or about 150 institutions—fit into that category. Since some of these are specialized institutions—military academies, music conservatories, and so on—the real number of colleges that take less than half their applicants is less than one hundred. Apply a more stringent definition to "selective"—accepting only one in three or one in four—and you're talking about roughly three dozen institutions.

When a college accepts everyone who is qualified, the admissions process is simple. Meet the minimum standards and you're in. State schools generally operate on this model, with a few variations. At the University of Wyoming, for instance, admission is guaranteed as long as you get passing marks in high school. More competitive state schools generally use a formula based on grades and/or standardized test scores. Essays, recommendations, and other paraphernalia are generally unnecessary except for applicants on the borderline. The message of all this? To paraphrase the old recruiting poster: American colleges and universities want YOU. No matter who you are, if you meet the minimum standards, there are a lot of colleges ready to offer you a first-rate education.

AT A FEW, THE COMPETITION INTENSIFIES

The dark lining to the silver cloud is the growing selectivity of the colleges at the top of the admissions ziggurat. They're the usual suspects in the growing national obsession with prestigious alma maters, the same few that accept a third or less of their applicants (see box, page 112). In the past ten years, applications to these schools have risen dramatically, making a once competitive situation border on the absurd. The deluge has been especially heavy at prestigious national universities: the Ivy League, Duke, Emory, Georgetown, Johns Hopkins, MIT, Northwestern, Notre Dame, Rice, Stanford, and Tufts, to name a few. For a recent freshman class, the admissions office at Harvard University received over 9,400 applications from students with SAT scores above 1400. It accepted fewer than 2,000, including many with lower scores who had other compelling qualifications. A recent report to high schools from Brown University revealed that fewer than half of the valedictorians who applied were accepted.

A handful of public universities have also entered the ranks of the highly selective elite—for out-of-state students. These universities include the University of Virginia, the University of Michigan, the University of North Carolina, the University of Texas, and the University of California at Berkeley and Los Angeles. The rise in applications at highbrow liberal arts colleges has been less steep, though notable gainers include elite Northeastern schools such as Smith, Swarthmore, and Wellesley, plus a smattering of others across the nation, including Davidson, Colorado College, and Pomona.

If you've set your sights on an elite school, join the club. Most of them will give you an outstanding education and open plenty of doors after graduation. But try to maintain some perspective, and avoid becoming another pathetic lamb following the herd. Just because a college attracts lots of applications doesn't mean it's the greatest place on earth. Some are overrated; others have become so crowded that they no longer deliver the quality education suggested by their name. Ask yourself if all the pressure is really worth it. Some people thrive on the challenge of the competitive college scramble; others suffer from anxiety, depression, anorexia, and worse. There are a lot of desperately unhappy people at the Harvards of the world, and a lot of others on the way to success and fulfillment at universities you've never heard of. The college search should be about picking the right school for you, not picking the most prestigious one you can get into. Don't end up like the student who described his time on a well-known but (for him) inappropriate campus as "serving a jail term with a $100,000 fine."

The Highly Selective Applicant Blues

	1986		1996	
COLLEGE	NUMBER OF APPLICATIONS	% ACCEPTED	NUMBER OF APPLICATIONS	% ACCEPTED
Amherst	4,580	21	4,680	19
Harvard	13,700	16	18,190	11
MIT	5,060	36	8,020	24
Northwestern	9,400	46	15,630	35
Penn	13,100	35	15,860	30
Princeton	12,660	17	14,870	11
Rice	3,840	31	7,000	22
Stanford	16,140	16	16,630	19
Swarthmore	2,450	38	4,010	30
Wellesley	2,420	52	3,310	42
Williams	4,660	25	5,061	24
Yale	11,740	19	12,950	18

THE ADMISSIONS PROCESS AT HIGHLY SELECTIVE SCHOOLS

If your resolve is still firm, hang on for the ride. The highly selective admissions process is complicated and subjective. The problem is that these schools are swamped with applications from many more qualified students than they can accept. Who can say how they should choose? Would you rather admit the tennis player with the 3.50 GPA or the concert violinist with the 3.49? How many math geniuses should be admitted for every artsy dilettante? And how many polite Midwesterners should there be to balance off all the pushy Easterners?

Under these circumstances, it's no surprise that desperate applicants will grasp at any straw to set themselves apart from the crowd. One applicant to Stanford took out a full page ad in the school paper begging the admissions office to admit him. An audacious University of Virginia applicant actually sent a shoe with the message: "Now that I have one foot in the door, I hope you'll let me have the other one." This little stratagem might have worked, but the other shoe dropped when nearby William and Mary received the exact same treatment—and compared notes with UVA. Though gimmicks like these can be amusing, they seldom work. The jaded eye of the admissions officer has seen most of them a thousand times.

Before you throw up your hands in despair, take heart. People who think the admissions process is arbitrary simply don't understand the logic. The purpose is not to assemble the best group of students. If that were the case, the college's libraries would be overflowing every night, but the gyms, concert halls, and yearbook offices would be vacant. Nor is the aim to

Straining Sal: A Parable for Stressed-Out Applicants

Just because a college is more selective doesn't mean it is a good fit for you. Consider the case of Straining Sal, a slightly above-average student who applied to thirteen highly selective colleges in the desperate hope that one might accept her. She finally got in off the wait list of her thirteenth choice—and spent the next four years struggling to keep her head above water competing with some of the smartest students in the country. Between review sessions, tutoring, and nonstop studying, poor Sal had no life. Meanwhile, her self-esteem took a severe beating as she constantly compared herself with students with much more ability than she would ever have. When it came time to look for a job, the prestigious name on the top of the diploma couldn't make up for Sal's low grades and her lack of extracurricular involvement. The last we heard, she was working at a local fast-food establishment.

How different her career might have been had she chosen the less-selective college that was right for her! There, she might have found the help she needed to overcome her academic weaknesses. With peers of similar ability, she might have had the chance to grow in self-confidence. Leadership opportunities would have come her way as she continued to blossom. By graduation, she could easily have compiled the combination of high grades and extracurricular involvement that is impressive to employers no matter what college one attends. Most important, she might actually have enjoyed her college experience and emerged from those years a more focused, mature young woman.

assemble a group of well-rounded students. Though every campus needs some, this kind of person tends to be reasonably good in many things but not a standout in any one. The true goal is to create a well-rounded community of individuals who each add a unique talent or characteristic to the mix. In the words of one admissions dean at an elite university: "We want a class of serious, bright, intellectually curious students that represents the many populations of our country in terms of geographical, economic, racial, ethnic, religious, and political characteristics. We seek students who pursue one or more school or nonschool activities through to levels of distinction. Special efforts are taken to enroll gifted writers, artists, athletes, and musicians, as well as those with diverse interests or experience in specific areas of study."

WHAT'S MY CATEGORY?

Picture life on a college campus and the various organizations that make it go. Each of these is an interest group that the admissions office must satisfy. The alumni office will lobby for the son of their recent million-dollar donor; the football coach will fight for the 300-pound noseguard he covets to shore up the defensive line; the multicultural-affairs coalition will be rioting in the streets if the number of minority students goes down. Instead of "What SAT scores do I need to get in?" a better question might be "What's my category?" Few admissions offices would admit to having quotas for the various "types" of students they seek, but practically all have rough guidelines for the number they want of each. The more students in your category, the more competition you'll face to win a spot in the class.

Though the system favors many subgroups that are in short supply, critics have charged "reverse discrimination," seizing upon the fact that some minority groups are accepted at a higher rate than other races. Lively debate continues in state legislatures and the legal system, and a few state universities have been forced to abandon policies that set aside scholarships or places in the class for certain races. Since private universities don't depend on taxpayer money, their policies are less likely to change. The quest for diversity has less to do with "affirmative action" than it does with the belief that educational communities are enriched by including students from different backgrounds. Though colleges have become more careful in specifying race as a factor in admissions, they can use other characteristics such as socioeconomic status to achieve the same result. The ideal of diversity continues to be one of the guiding principles for assembling a class.

With all the clamor over favoritism to minorities, an equal preference

The Category Game: Your Chances

Here are the approximate acceptance rates for different "types" of applicants. The numbers are for a hypothetical private college that accepts 30 percent, but the logic applies equally to most highly selective schools.

All applicants	30%
Recruited athletes	75%
Underrepresented minorities	60%
Alumni children	50%
"Typical" applicants	15%

for children of alumni and major donors goes largely unnoticed. Many colleges will bend over backward for such applicants; if the admissions office thinks they can muddle through till graduation, they're in. Some colleges help the offspring of wealthy alums sneak in the side door by allowing them to transfer in after a year at another school. Since most colleges don't publicize the academic credentials of transfers, they can take weak students without destroying their SAT profiles.

The logic of the categories also holds for students who are not in one of the sought-after subgroups. Though yearbook editor or student council representative is a nice activity to put on your list, it hardly sets you apart from the crowd. But if you edit a publication on Jewish culture or are president of a citywide teenage chess players' society, that's a little more eye-catching. Similarly, admission is always slightly more difficult if you declare yourself a premed, because countless thousands of others do the same thing every year. Though applicants should never try to mold themselves into a phony image, it pays to accentuate elements of your record that set you off from the crowd.

One other category that isn't much talked about is what we dub "the underdog factor." Admissions offices dearly love candidates who come from underprivileged backgrounds or who have overcome great obstacles. After sifting through hordes of well-coached, well-manicured applicants, admissions officers find this type of student refreshing. If you fall into that category, don't let any admissions numbers intimidate you. Your special qualifications will get their due.

For those of you quaking in your shoes because you're not a star quarterback or a state symphony tuba player, we repeat: The above applies only to a handful of supercompetitive schools. Most less-selective private-colleges mimic the same process, but their applicant pools are not stronge-nough for them to be nearly as choosy. At the vast majority of colleges, you don't need to be a superstar to get in.

A final variable that has become increasingly important in the 1990s is a family's ability to pay the bill. Many colleges, hungry for tuition dollars,

---

Admissions Officers: Who Are They?

The typical admissions officer (or AO, as they are known) is not at all like the academic stuffed shirt that most high school students imagine. AOs tend to be young, friendly, outgoing, and idealistic. They genuinely enjoy working with high school students— otherwise they wouldn't be in the profession—and they don't mind (much) the fact that they are always underpaid. Most admissions offices include a professional staff of about ten to fifteen people. Recent college graduates (often from the institution where they work) generally make up about half the staff. Many of these people will stay in admissions for two or three years before moving on to graduate or professional school. Anyone with more than five years' experience is a veteran in the field; even most directors are young, usually in their thirties or forties.

The life of an AO includes three primary tasks: recruiting, inter-viewing, and evaluating the applications. Most offices assign their staff to particular regions of the country. From September through November, most AOs are on the road visiting a selection of high schools determined largely by the previous year's applications. A high school visit is often the first time an applicant gets to meet an AO in the flesh. Though not a substitute for campus interviews, a high school visit can be a useful introduction to the college search. (See your guidance counselor in the early fall of your senior year for a list of the representatives visiting your school.)

Crunch time for the admissions office is January through April, when most of the applications flood in. The grueling pace during these months is one of the reasons that the admissions field has such a high rate of burnout. How would you like to wake up every morning with the knowledge that you had to read a hundred appli-cant files before going to bed?

---

give preference to applicants with low financial need. The impact on admission chances is minor at the most selective (and richest) colleges, but those on the next rungs of the ladder often use ability to pay as an key determinant of who gets admitted. We offer a fuller discussion of the impact of financial aid on the admissions process in Chapter 18.

How They Decide

How do admissions offices evaluate applications? Very carefully. From the moment an applicant makes initial contact, generally in the junior year, a file is created in his or her name. When the applicant comes for an interview, a report is added to the file. Standardized test reports, teacher recommendations, and transcripts all find their way inside, and when the student sends the completed application (with fee), the file is complete.

Though admissions offices are formed in a committee structure, much of their work is done individually. Colleges usually divide up the applications geographically according to the regional responsibilities of each staff member. At this stage, the admissions officer spends an average of, say, five to ten minutes reading each application. Most schools use a two-part rating system for (1) academic and (2) nonacademic factors. The science nerd with the 4.0 GPA might be a 1E—great academics, lousy extracurricular/personal. The All-American football player who can barely read might be a 5A. After the initial evaluation, most applications are read a second time by another admissions officer. If the verdict is a clear-cut admit or deny, the application will probably be sent to the dean or director for final action.

Most admissions committees include university faculty—sometimes as full-fledged members, more often as expert evaluators in their fields. The tape submitted by an aspiring French horn player is sent to the music department; the line drawings from the budding designer go to the art department. Coaches also get into the act, generally with a list of applicants they want for their teams. (A hint for athletes: Get the coach on your side!) Most university presidents do not involve themselves in the fate of particular applicants, but many have indirect ways of making their interests known.

The borderline cases, which can cause protracted haggling, are put off until the end for consideration by the full committee. If your application is in the last batch, all the rating systems go out the window, and there's no telling what will decide your fate. How adamantly will the admissions officer that interviewed you argue your case? What will the art professor think of the slides you submitted? Will you be one of the dean's "wild card" admits that he saves for students denied by the committee as a whole?

Talk about a cliff hanger!

9
Shaping Your Record

On your day of reckoning with the admissions committee, one factor is most likely to determine your fate: the high school transcript. Unlike essays or SATs, the transcript is a four-year chronicle of your ability, work ethic, and involvement. No amount of cramming, coaching, or fast talking can make it better. That's why admissions officers will consider it the key ingredient in evaluating your potential for success as a college student. After all, the best predictor of how a person will perform in the future is how he or she performed in similar situations in the past.

There are really two elements to your record in high school. The academic transcript—your courses and grades—is by far the most important. Also significant at highly selective schools is your list of extracurricular involvements, including offices held and time committed. Together, they paint a portrait that gives admissions officers detailed insight into just about every character trait you can think of.

A TALE OF TWO STUDENTS

Though admissions policies vary widely across the many types of colleges and universities, the primacy of the transcript is universal. Admissions officers want the answers to three questions:

1. What are your grades?
2. Have you taken the most challenging courses?
3. Are your grades improving or declining?

The importance of your grades is hardly front-page news, but many students are fixated with getting a high grade point average and don't understand how thoroughly admissions officers will scrutinize their course selections and grade trend. To illustrate, we take a peek inside the lives of two aspiring applicants, Charlene and Charlie.

Charlene is the kind of student teachers love—always doing the homework, always asking a question when she doesn't understand. Because of her weak background from middle school, ninth and tenth grade were a struggle. But her improvement has been steady, and she has been fearless in tackling tough courses even in her worst subjects. She has enrolled in two College Board Advanced Placement courses each in her junior and senior years, including the ones in her favorite subjects (calculus and physics) and her least favorite subjects (English and Spanish). As a senior, her overall GPA has climbed to 3.37—a solid B+—which gives her a rank of 73rd in her class of 250.

And then there's Charlie. He's a fun-loving kind of guy with a quick wit and loads of intelligence. He also seems to have an internal homing device for the easiest possible path through high school. His transcript is crowded with less-then-challenging, semi-academic courses such as Physical Education for the Twenty-first Century: Getting a Head Start on the Battle of the Bulge. As a junior and senior, he has opted out of the really tough courses, quitting math after Algebra II and loading up on the one subject he really likes, history. Partly because of his course selection, Charlie's GPA is a spiffy 3.97. With only two Bs on his whole transcript, Charlie ranks 4th in his class of 98.

So which of our two applicants wins in the highly selective admissions race? Sorry, Charlie, this one is a no-brainer. Admissions committees can see through your charade; they know nobody twisted your arm to take those three study halls instead of physics and pre-calculus. And as for that Sociology of Sports course, pleeeeease! In the words of George Stoner of George Washington University, "So-called gut courses taken to fatten a grade average are as easy to spot as cosmetic transcript decoration and equally easy to discount."

On the other hand, Charlene gets major points for tackling the tough courses. "I'd rather see a B, or even an occasional C, in an AP course than an A in an easy course. This is why we do not make decisions based only upon grade point averages," says Ann Wright of Smith College. Almost as important as Charlene's course selection is her upward grade trend. The more recent the grades, the more important they become. A lot of freshman mistakes can be forgiven if there are high grades in the junior and senior year.

KNOW YOUR GOALS

As the tale of Charlene and Charlie makes clear, highly challenging courses on your transcript are a big plus (aside from their value as a learning experience).

How many honors and AP courses are enough? If you're eyeing a highly selective college, you should probably take as many Advanced Placement courses as you can manage without harming your grades or extracurricular involvement. At the Ivy League and its cousins, nothing less than top grades in most or all of the advanced courses will get you a foot in the door.

If your school doesn't offer AP courses, don't fret. The trick is to take the most challenging courses available, whatever they might be. If you come from a supercompetitive school, your record will also be evaluated in context. Be sure to challenge yourself, but rest assured that colleges will evaluate your GPA and class rank in light of your school's strength.

Your academic interests will also affect course selection. If you want to be a pre-med, taking plenty of upper-level science courses is mandatory. But also pay attention to related disciplines. Prospective business majors are advised to take plenty of math. "You'll definitely need four years, preferably through calculus," says Nanette Clift of the B-school at Washington University. Ditto for future engineers. If in doubt as to your course selection, consult with your guidance counselor or call the colleges on your preliminary list.

To really stand out in the most selective pools, it helps to find ways of going beyond the standard curriculum. If you've exhausted your school's physics program, take an advanced course at a nearby college. If you finish integral calculus as a junior, work with a teacher to design your own independent study in multivariable equations. To be a scholar in Harvard or Amherst's applicant pool, you'll need to show self-sustaining intellectual

Preferred High School Curriculum for Applicants to Selective Colleges

English	4 years
Math	3 years (through Algebra II)
Natural sciences	3 years (including chemistry or physics)
Social studies	3 years
Foreign language	3 years

energy that seeks new challenges in addition to completing all the "right" courses.

Different rules apply to students who are aiming for a large state university. These schools attract tens of thousands of applicants each year, and as a result they often rely on formulas for grades and test scores to make their admissions decisions. (See Chapter 8, "Inside the Admissions Process.") Unfortunately, GPA at these schools often *is* more important than the level of the courses (as long as they are college prep).

For most students, moderation in advanced and AP courses is the wisest counsel. As the hype builds for admission to elite colleges, some students overload themselves with too many APs—and then suffer the consequences of lower grades and major stress. Follow your interests and challenge yourself, but don't feel pressured to take every AP course in the book.

EXTRACURRICULARS, JOBS, AND SUMMER PROGRAMS

Though not as important as the transcript, an impressive record of extracurricular achievement can be a significant factor in admissions success. The more selective a college, the more likely extracurricular involvements will play a significant role. As we illustrated in Chapter 3, the emphasis should be on quality instead of quantity. Try to pick activities at which you can excel or in which you can acquire leadership positions, and then stick with them through your entire high school career. When possible, enter contests or take on extra projects that will hone your skills and win recognition.

Instead of doing the extracurricular scene, some students take a part-time job. Which looks better? The answer varies. The best reason to take a job is to help pay family expenses; any college would look with favor on that. Flipping burgers in a fast-food joint to buy yourself a new Harley is a less compelling use of your time. The more responsibility a job allows you, the more impressive it will look in the eyes of the admissions office.

Since time immemorial, college interviewers have asked, "What did you do last summer?" There is no right answer to the question; the main idea is to avoid having to report that you sat around watching *Gilligan's Island* reruns.

An increasingly popular option is to attend a summer program at a college or university. In addition to sampling college-level work, students get a six-week trial of life as a college student. A college summer program can be an excellent option, as long as there are no illusions that summer attendance at a highly selective school will help you get in as a degree student. It usually doesn't, unless you happen to establish a relationship with a professor who goes to bat for you.

Other perfectly good ways to spend a summer include a wilderness experience, an athletic camp, a service project (at home or abroad), or some comparable experience. Travel can be valuable, especially if it includes exposure to a foreign language. When possible, use your summer to build on skills or deepen interests that you already possess. Most important of all, have fun!

10
How Important Is the SAT?

The SAT casts a long shadow over the selective college admissions process. To hear some people tell it, the SAT is the be-all and end-all of everything: the deciding factor on whether you get into a good school and the litmus test of your worth as an individual. "What did you get on the SAT?" will be the eternal question from test day forward, and when you die, your scores will be etched forever on your tombstone.

Or will they? Is the SAT really as important as people think? The answer—as unsatisfactory as this may sound—is "yes and no." At some schools, the SAT is merely one of at least a half dozen factors that play a significant role. At others, it is pretty darned important. Perhaps David Erdmann of Rollins College said it best: "At most institutions, standardized test scores count less than the students think and more than the colleges are willing to admit."

A NUMBER FOR YOUR THOUGHTS

The allure of standardized testing to measure academic ability is easy to understand: It provides a simple way of making comparisons among students. No matter what high school you go to, or what courses you take, the standardized tests put you on the same scale as millions of other students after three short hours of taking a test.

The New PSAT: The Latest Round in the Battle of the Sexes

The fall of 1996 witnessed another skirmish in the College Board's never-ending war against charges of gender discrimination. That's the story behind the new writing section added to the Preliminary SAT (PSAT). The test's traditional math and verbal sections have been scaled back to make room for multiple-choice questions that mirror those on the SAT II Writing Test. Why? Because girls tend to do better on writing questions than boys.

The College Board's gender problem is as old as the SAT: While girls tend to get better grades than boys in school, boys do better than girls on standardized tests. The problem is particularly acute in the case of the PSAT because it is the qualifying test for the National Merit Scholarship Program. Does the fact that more boys than girls win them mean that the competition discriminates against girls? The College Board and National Merit Committee certainly act as if it does. First, they created the "Selection Index"—which doubles the verbal score relative to the math—as the scholarship qualifier. That ensured more female Merit Scholars, but the goal of 50–50 representation remains elusive. There is only one thing certain about the latest round of controversy: the College Board and its critics will both live to fight another day.

The full name for what people know as "the SAT" has been changed to the "SAT I: Reasoning Test," but it still consists of math and verbal portions. The subject-area exams formerly called "Achievement Tests" are now referred to as "SAT II: Subject Tests." The SAT I is the only standardized test that purports to measure overall academic aptitude, or what the College Board now calls "developed ability." Most highly selective colleges require the SAT I, and many also mandate up to three SAT II Subject Tests. As an alternative to the SAT I and II, a student can generally choose to submit scores from the ACT, a test administered by a different company that includes sections on English, Math, Reading, and Science Reasoning. Use of the ACT is most prevalent among southern and western state universities and less-selective private colleges.

The SAT I and II are developed by the College Board, a giant testing-and-research organization known by its characteristic acorn-and-oak-leaf symbol. The Educational Testing Service (ETS) is an affiliated company that administers the tests.

THE SAT'S FLAWS

Though the College Board doesn't like to admit it, standardized testing (and the SAT in particular) has a sordid past. The forerunner of today's SAT was developed in the 1920s by a Princeton professor whose chief concern was weeding out "feebleminded" ethnic groups from the American gene pool.

SAT–ACT Conversion Chart

Here is how scores on one correlate to the other. If you get a 23 on the ACT, for example, that's roughly the same as getting a 1060 on the SAT.

ACT	SAT		ACT	SAT
36	1600		22	1030
35	1580		21	990
34	1530		20	950
33	1460		19	910
32	1410		18	860
31	1360		17	820
30	1320		16	770
29	1280		15	720
28	1240		14	670
27	1210		13	600
26	1170		12	540
25	1140		11	480
24	1100		10	430
23	1060		1–9	400

Source: College Board.

Back then, you could measure intelligence and put a single number on it. The modern discipline of psychology has shown intelligence to be far more complicated, but the SAT, which developed out of the original notion, lives on. Meanwhile, studies have shown that the high school transcript is a better predictor of academic performance than standardized tests. In the words of one selective college admissions officer, "You just cannot equate three years of high school with one three-hour test on a Saturday morning."

In recent years, the College Board and the SAT have been under siege on a variety of fronts. Charges have been leveled that the SAT discriminates on the basis of race, sex, and socioeconomic background. Another problem is the reality that private coaching may increase scores. With SAT prep a burgeoning industry, many observers believe that scores depend to some extent on how well a student has been drilled. If that is so, they may merely assess skill in taking a particular test rather than intelligence or ability. (See Chapter 11, "How to Prepare for Standardized Tests.") Finally, the College Board made a questionable decision to "recenter" the test in 1995. The average scores had sunk to 430 and 480, so they were hiked to 500 and 500. The new scale means that historical comparisons are harder. If Big Sis scored 1000 on the test five years ago, you'll need an 1100 to match her. On the high end, however, an 800 is far easier to get than it once was.

WHERE THE SAT HAS CLOUT

The schools that generally put the most emphasis on the SAT are large state universities. Many of them must accept all "qualified" in-state applicants, and the easiest way to adhere to that mandate is to use SAT and grade-point cutoffs. Scores typically make up a fourth to a half of the "acceptance formulas" at these schools.

A second category of institution where the SAT and other standardized tests carry weight is technical institutes. "At highly selective institutions of engineering, math and science scores must be within certain ranges in order for a student to be competitive," says one dean.

A third type of school that often puts added weight on scores is the small liberal arts college that is struggling to maintain enrollment—or trying to climb the selectivity ladder. Many of these are reluctant to accept students with low SATs because the college's score profile—and hence its place in the rankings—will suffer.

How Accurate Are SAT I Scores?

Not very.

Test makers don't exactly shout about it from the hills, but when pressed, they concede that standardized admissions tests are far from precise.

Take your SAT score, for example. There's one chance in three that the 550 that arrived in the little envelope from ETS should really be at least 580 or no more than 520. There's one chance in ten that it should be either in the low 600s or the high 400s.

Here's why.

The SAT can't measure everything that you know (like your entire vocabulary) in one Saturday morning. So by necessity, every test is a *sample* of your academic knowledge and ability, and the nature of this sample varies with every edition of the test. The variation, for purely statistical reasons, is what is known as the "standard error of measurement" (SEM).

The SEM on the SAT I is 30 points. Since roughly 1.8 million students take the SAT I every year, this means that about 600,000 reported scores are off by at least 30 points and 180,000 are off by at least 60 points. And this doesn't include test-day influences, such as the fact that you may have arrived at the site with a headache.

The margin of error can be illustrated graphically. Suppose 60 students have reported scores of 580. According to the laws of statistics, their "true" scores will break down as follows:

520 or below	520–550	550–580	580–610	610–640	640 or above
3	7	20	20	7	3

College admissions officers—the good ones, at least—understand this. That's why they don't pay much attention to score differences of 30 or 40 points.

Neither should you.

Students who are not satisfied with their SAT I scores should probably take the ACT for another chance to do well on a standardized test. Since the pool of students that take the ACT is less competitive, percentile scores will probably be higher.

WHERE IT DOESN'T

At the opposite end of the spectrum are schools that have stopped requiring standardized tests altogether. The staunchest antitest institutions tend to be liberal arts colleges with a slightly alternative approach to education. For philosophical reasons, they reject any standardized tests to measure academic potential.

A recent minitrend has featured a handful of more mainstream liberal arts colleges that have decided to make the SAT I optional, though they generally require SAT IIs or the ACT. "Connecticut College has come to the conclusion that the SAT—and the cottage industry that has grown up around it—no longer serves students well," declared Claire Mathews in announcing CC's optional–SAT I policy. According to William Hiss of Bates College, the nonsubmitters tend to be women, minorities, and "every subgroup you could imagine that is being hammered by standardized tests." A policy of SAT I optional has the added fringe benefit of allowing colleges to accept low scorers without reporting that they do so. Since many observers already believe that SAT II Subject Tests are a better predictor of academic success than SAT I, SAT I optional is a trend to watch in the years ahead.

THE GREAT MIDDLE

Finally, there is the great middle: schools where standardized test scores are important but not that important (or something like that).

At most colleges, test scores are one of a range of factors used in making admissions decisions. Rarely are they as critical as the transcript. Test scores tend to take on larger importance only when they are out of line with the grade point average. Exceptionally high scores coupled with low-grades may signal students who haven't applied themselves very seriously

Selective Schools That Do Not Require SAT I or ACT Scores

Antioch College
Bard College
Bates College
Bowdoin College
Bradford College
Connecticut College
Dickinson College
Franklin and Marshall College
Goddard College
Hampshire College

Lafayette College
Lewis and Clark College
Middlebury College
Muhlenberg College
St. John's College (Maryland and
  New Mexico)
Union College
Ursinus College
Wheaton College

and will probably continue this pattern in college. So don't count on acing the SAT as a way to make up for four years of goofing off in high school. "We will always take a student with strong school performance and weak scores over someone with weak performance and strong scores," says Steven Syverson of Lawrence University.

Though it obviously helps to have high scores, the critical thing is to fall in the college's general range. Don't be too concerned about median or mean scores. (See Chapter 5, "Cutting Through the Propaganda.") At most colleges you're in good shape if you're between the 25th and 75th percentile of the school's SAT profile. At the elite, you'll need to be at the median or better in the absence of consideration in a special category.

THE BOTTOM LINE

In the foreseeable future, the SAT will continue to hold sway over the lives of aspiring college applicants. Admissions officers understand its flaws and hate the idea of pegging applicants with a single number, but to get rid of the SAT is politically impossible at most colleges. "You have to sit in the chair of an admissions officer to understand the pressures to keep the numbers up," says Thomas Anthony, former director of admissions at Colgate University. "Presidents and faculty don't give a darn about what class rank looks like, but they light up when your scores increase by five points. This is how the nation measures academic quality." All too many colleges publicly downplay their use of the SAT in admissions even though it continues to be an important factor in most decisions.

What is all boils down to: Don't take the SAT or any standardized test too seriously or too lightly. As with any other important test, you should do your best but should also realize that it isn't the end of the world if the kid down the street gets a better score. Your worth as a human being—or as a potential freshman—cannot be reduced to a three-digit number. After all, when was the last time you saw a tombstone with SAT scores inscribed on it?

How to Prepare for Standardized Tests

An old sales pitch for lottery tickets once proclaimed, "All you need is a dollar and a dream."

In the world of standardized test prep, all you need is $1,000 and a dream. That's how much you'll pay (almost) for a few weeks of intensive work with a brand-name prep company. Their sales pitch is attractive—"guaranteed" score increases—but the reality is a little more iffy. Some students' scores go up drastically after taking a prep course, and these people swear by them. But other students score about the same or even go down (and seldom broadcast that fact).

Instead of blindly following the herd, think seriously about whether a prep course meets your particular needs. The road to successful standardized testing begins long before you sit down to blacken ovals on a Saturday morning. In order to find out where you stand, you'll need to cover the basics of test prep on your own.

GET AN EARLY START

Everybody agrees that the *best* way to prepare is to work hard in school. Lots of reading and good conversation with intelligent people (maybe even your parents) round out the long-term recipe for success. Some high schools offer free or discounted prep courses that can help you begin preparation in earnest. About six months before test day, consider buying a couple of prep books, or check out similar material available on disk, CD-ROM, or the Internet (see Chapter 7, "Where to Learn More," page 98). Take one of the diagnostic tests to locate your strengths and weaknesses, then prepare accordingly. Familiarize yourself with the test format so you won't need to

Savvy Test-Taking: the Basics

<u>Answer the Easy Questions First</u> An easy question is worth the same as a hard one. If you're stumped, mark the question and move on. The time invested in solving a single hard one is better used on four or five easy ones.

<u>Mark Your Answer Sheet with Care</u> If you get to question 40 in your test booklet and notice that the answer sheet says 41, you're in trouble. It pays to double-check the numbers—especially if you skip any questions.

<u>Know Your Calculator</u> Virtually any four-function, scientific, or graphing calculator can be used for the PSAT, ACT, SAT I, and SAT II Math IC and 2C. Nothing fancy here—all you'll need are simple functions. Just be sure you have plenty of practice with it so as to avoid wasting time.

<u>Guessing is Good</u> If you can eliminate one or more wrong answers, you should guess. Since you get one point for every right answer and lose only a quarter of a point for each wrong one, educated guessing raises your score. Random guessing neither helps nor hurts on the SATs. By contrast, the ACT has no penalty for wrong answers, and thus even random guessing helps.

<u>Watch for Tricks</u> If you find a question that appears strangely easy—especially after a string of hard ones—it is probably a trap. This is especially true in math, where every question assesses a concept or thought process. If you find yourself saying, "Ahh, *that's* what they want," you're probably on the right track.

spend time reading directions when test day comes. Lastly, take as many practice tests as you can stomach to get accustomed to the grueling pace.

SAT I   The verbal part focuses primarily on two things: vocabulary and reading comprehension. The vocabulary is where preparation makes the most headway. A disciplined approach of thirty vocabulary words a night will almost certainly result in improved scores. The best approach is to familiarize yourself with as many words and definitions as possible rather than slaving to memorize definitions word for word. You don't need to recite the definition—you merely need to recall it when you see the word in the context of a question.

On the reading comprehension, the best prep is to practice, practice, practice. Reading comprehension often boils down to a test of concentration. Applicants who do poorly often suffer from the I-just-read-the-paragraph-and-don't-remember-a-word syndrome. For the math part, you should definitely brush up on the types of equations you are likely to see. Remember that the SAT I is called a "reasoning" test, not a "computation" test. The emphasis will be on problem-solving ingenuity rather than endless calculations.

Every student applying to selective colleges should take at least one SAT I in the spring of their junior year. Some counselors recommend taking it twice as a junior—generally in March and May—on the theory that students do better the second time when the first is still fresh in their minds. This approach leaves applicants well positioned to explore early-decision or early-action programs. Many students will want to take a second or third SAT I in the fall of the senior year.

SAT II and the ACT The secret to doing your best on the SAT II is timing. Since the tests cover academic subjects, the best time to take them is at the end of the most relevant course (the June date at the end of your junior year is usually the optimal one). Though you can take up to three SAT IIs at a single administration, the best strategy is to spread them out to ensure adequate preparation and avoid fatigue. Too many applicants wait until the fall of their senior year to pack in all of their SAT IIs. One test that you probably *should* put off until the senior year is the SAT II in Writing, a skill that will improve throughout your high school years.

The right preparation for the ACT is also likely to improve your score. Since the ACT includes four subject areas, diagnosis of your strengths and

SAT II: Subject Tests

Writing	Chinese
Literature	French
American History and Social Studies	German
World History	Modern Hebrew
Math Level I (with or without calculator)	Italian
Math Level II (with calculator)	Japanese
Biology	Latin
Chemistry	Spanish
Physics	English Language Proficiency

weaknesses is key. As for timing, we recommend May or June of the junior year, with a second administration in October or December, if necessary.

BIG BUCKS AND BIGGER PROMISES

Having sampled the tried-and-true methods of preparation, some applicants may want to consider spending between $500 and $1,000 to let a private coaching firm cast its magic spell. At some elite private schools, well over half the students lay down their money. Only you can decide if a prep course is worth the price. We think the answer is often found in careful reflection about your motives and how you learn best.

There are two gremlins that test-prep agencies count on to deliver most of their customers: fear and guilt. The fear is that the boy down the street will get ahead of you because he is prepping, and the guilt is what your parents would feel if they didn't do everything possible to help you get in. Even though they may be uncertain of the benefits, many families succumb to the philosophy of "it can't hurt." But an extra $1,000 seems a lot to pay for peace of mind, especially when you can buy the book that includes all the techniques for about $15.

Regardless of claims to the contrary, top students seldom get much benefit from coaching. The effortless insight that marks the best standardized-test takers cannot be taught. Nor will a prep course do much good for a student who lacks motivation; a better strategy for these students is to sleep with a prep book under the pillow (much cheaper and just as effective). Finally, those for whom test prep has become a neurotic obsession—or a parental crusade—are advised to chill out. Compulsively pursuing a higher score seldom works.

For diligent students, the prospects for a prep course vary. Those with organization and initiative will probably do just as well with books or software. A more likely candidate is a good student who is befuddled by standardized tests. The number-one determinant of SAT success is confidence, and if you think a prep course will give you more, do it.

Other types who may benefit include:

Students Who Are Enthusiastic About a Prep Course   If you believe that it will work, the odds are greater that it will.

Students with Mediocre Preparation   Improvement comes where there is room for improvement.

Students Who Learn Best with Adult Direction These include step-by-step learners who like to ask questions and students who need help in staying focused.

Before you sign up at a particular agency, find out exactly what you'll be learning. Is the emphasis on vocabulary words and equations? Or on test-taking strategies? How long is the course? As a rule, longer courses have the most impact. Pay no attention to guarantees. These merely mean that if your scores don't improve, you get a free second helping of what didn't work the first time.

If you are thinking seriously about a coaching course, try to do it before the first time you take the test. That way, you'll avoid an upward blip in your score between the first and second time you take it. If you happen to improve a great deal the second time after being coached, this could raise suspicion that your score is artificially high—the result of a cram course. If you do take the test without prepping and are disappointed, you can still consider a prep course. Blip or not, a high score is better than a low one.

How Many Times Should I Take the SAT I?

Either two or three times. Because of the standard error of measurement (SEM), once is generally not enough (unless you shoot the moon). Many colleges consider your highest verbal and highest math even if they come from different test dates. But if you take it more than three times, you risk looking like an obsessed geek with nothing better to do than worry about your SAT scores. Also remember that score reporting for the SAT I is cumulative. Each time one score is reported, all are reported.

Most students should take it the first time in January, March, or May of their junior year. Some counselors recommend taking it twice among those dates, believing that students who take two in quick succession are likely to do better the second time. (This approach also sets you up to apply for early-decision or early-action.) Most students will want to take it once more in October, November, or December of their senior year.

THE COLLEGES SQUIRM

The growing popularity of SAT prep courses has put the colleges in an embarrassing position. The possibility that coaching can manipulate a supposedly objective pillar of the admissions process is bad enough. Even worse is the fact that only people with money have access. "I promote professionally the ETS stand that coaching is limited in its results—then I go off the record and say it depends on the student," says one admissions dean who prefers not be identified. If you do take an SAT prep course, you'll probably want to keep it under your hat when dealing with the admissions office. Though such courses are an accepted part of admissions, they are a subject the colleges prefer not to think about. (The College Board spent years denying that coaching could have any benefit. It now sells products to help coach you.)

In an ideal world, every high school student could prep for the SAT with a copy of *Moby Dick* and a good dictionary. Until that day comes, prep courses will be a viable alternative. They cost a pretty penny, but if you think your scores can improve from taking one, there is no reason why you shouldn't consider it.

12
Should I Be an Early Bird?

Early decision is a hot topic among today's college applicants. Faced with increasingly long odds for admission to the nation's elite schools, many students are trying to beat the odds by securing an early acceptance, and many colleges are encouraging the trend. At the nation's top Eastern prep schools, more than half of the students apply early, and the trend is spreading to Main Street U.S.A. Should I apply early? Will it help my chances? What if I get deferred? Inquiring applicants want to know.

The early programs come in two basic varieties: Early decision (ED) and early action (EA). Both require students to apply by an early deadline, generally November 1 or 15, and the college renders its decision by approximately December 15. (Borderline students may be "deferred" for consideration with the regular applicant pool.) Early decision is by far the most common of the two and requires applicants to make a firm commitment to enroll if accepted. Early action (EA), offered by only a handful of elite schools, requires no such commitment.

We'll say a few words about EA at the end of the chapter, but our primary focus is on the tens of thousands who apply via ED. A lot of hype has gone into promoting ED. Yes, it does give you a boost in admissions—but there are numerous pitfalls along the way. Though ED is right for some students, it is definitely the wrong move for others. We begin with an examination of the colleges' motives and then outline some of the pros and cons.

WHY THE COLLEGES WANT *YOU* (TO APPLY ED)

Appearances to the contrary, the colleges do not offer early decision merely to ease the stress in your life as a college applicant. Like glossy brochures and "cooked" SAT profiles, early decision is a way for the colleges to compete for students. At most colleges, less than half of those admitted by regular decision will choose to enroll. As students continue applying to more and more schools, uncertainty as to who will show up is increasing. Colleges know that ED applicants are in the bag, helping them to predict and control enrollment.

Another trade secret: Early decision allows colleges to make themselves appear more selective. The more students a college accepts ED, the fewer acceptances it needs to mail out to fill its class. If 100 percent of the ED applicants enroll and only 50 percent of the regular applicants enroll, a college would need to send twice as many acceptances to the regular applicants to get the same enrollment.

Another hidden motive for financially strapped colleges is the fact that most ED applicants tend to be from upper-income brackets. These students tend to be better informed and more likely to come from high-powered schools that prime them to apply early decision. Most colleges jump at the chance to lock in ED students who will not need financial aid.

With all these incentives, it is hardly surprising that colleges have been adding early-decision options left and right. In addition to the traditional November deadline, many colleges now offer an Early Decision II option in January or February. It goes without saying that applicants should be wary of the hard sell. The more desperate the college is for students, the more arm twisting you're likely to get.

EARLY DECISION BALANCE SHEET

Pitfalls

From the moment you mail the application, there's no turning back. You can apply ED to only one school, and if it accepts you, all other applications must be withdrawn. If you try to wriggle out of an early-decision commitment, you'll excite the wrath of the jilted college, which might try to locate your new suitor school and inform it of your shenanigans. If that happens, both colleges might rescind their offers.

Unfortunately, many students are stampeded into applying early instead of making a well-informed choice. "Along about mid-October, something I call early fever hits," says Wynne Curry, a college counselor at Seven Hills School in Cincinnati. "The seniors get very nervous and think, 'Oh, I should be applying somewhere early.' " The logic should be reversed: Only after a clear first choice has emerged should students consider ED. Even when applicants do think carefully about ED, it shortens the time they get to weigh their options. For a seventeen-year-old, the six-month period between November and April is a long time.

Applicants to ED programs at highly selective schools are often enticed by higher acceptance rates for the early round. But the percentage accepted via ED at the Ivy League and its cousins overstates the advantage. Reason? The early applicants to these schools are generally stronger than the regular admissions candidates.

Another pitfall regards financial aid. At a time when financial-aid packages are highly negotiable, ED prevents applicants from seeing more than one offer. The colleges use merit scholarships as recruiting tools, so they have little incentive to offer them to students already committed through ED. "If students apply early, the colleges don't have to fight as hard to get them," observes Jill Caskey of Paideia School in Atlanta.

Potential ED applicants should remember that college admissions is not a contest to see who can get the first acceptance. Picking the right school, whether in November or in April, is what matters.

Benefits

If you really do have a foolproof, ironclad, cross-your-heart-and-hope-to-die first choice, early decision could be worth considering. ED began as a way to help applicants avoid five months of nail biting between filing an application and receiving a decision. When you have an acceptance from First Choice U. in hand, the second semester can be a joyous time instead of a countdown to Judgment Day.

On a more practical level, ED will give you a slight advantage at top schools and a significant advantage at less selective ones. "Applying early

> *The odds are long for deferred early-decision or early-action candidates. On average, about one in ten is admitted.*

really can make a difference, especially if you're a perfectly qualified applicant but don't have a hook to single you out," says Susan Case of prestigious Milton Academy in Massachusetts. Colleges also value what one admissions dean calls "the loyalty factor." They would much prefer to enroll students who really want to be there (as demonstrated by an early commitment) rather than others who come only because they were denied admission at other schools. As a rule, the lower the college's "yield" on accepted applicants (the percentage of those accepted who actually enroll), the bigger the boost your admission chances will be given when you apply early.

Finally some candidates will find a financial-aid bonus from applying early. Though they won't be able to compare aid offers, they may benefit from special deals offered to encourage early-decision applicants. For instance, Dickinson College offers a guarantee to ED admits that the grant portion of their financial-aid package will never be reduced. At Franklin and Marshall, ED students get lower tuition and first choice in course selection and housing assignments. Many colleges unable to meet the full need of all their applicants will give first dibs on financial-aid money to those admitted ED. From a financial point of view, ED can be helpful if you get one of these deals. If not, it could be a bad move.

To sum up, early decision is probably a good idea for borderline students with low financial need who have a clear first choice. Others should be more cautious.

EARLY ACTION

While applying early decision is a serious step, early action requires much less agonizing. If you have a first choice that offers early action and you feel that you are a strong candidate, you might as well take the plunge. You're under no obligation, and you generally get until May 1 to make a final decision. Unfortunately, the number of schools offering early action is small.

Early action is more likely to be offered by big-name schools that have no problem getting applicants to sign on the dotted line. (A partial list includes Brown, the University of Chicago, Georgetown, Harvard, and

Timetable for First-Round Early Decision and Early Action

JUNIOR YEAR

January–May: Take ACT and/or SAT I.
June: If required, take SAT IIs.

Work hard! The junior year will be the last included in your transcript before decision time.

SENIOR YEAR

September–October: Work on applications. Hand out teacher recommendation forms. File early-decision or early-action applications according to deadlines. Take SAT or ACT if necessary. Register to receive the College Board's Financial Aid Profile if necessary.

November: Continue filing early-decision or early-action applications. Follow up with teacher recommendations. Continue working on regular-decision applications and taking standardized tests. File the Financial Aid Profile form, if necessary.

December–February: Receive notification. If you are accepted early-decision, you *must* withdraw all other applications.

MIT.) Interest in early action at these schools (especially Harvard) has exploded in recent years, but be warned that competition in the early pool at these schools is *fierce*. If there is a chance that your credentials will improve during the first semester of your senior year, it is best not to apply early to these or any other schools.

A final note for both early decision and early action. Start early! The deadlines will come sooner than you think!

13
How to Size Up a Campus

Visting campuses should be the most exciting stage of the college search. After months of hearing secondhand reports, this is your chance to see real college students in their native habitat and get a taste of the lifestyle that awaits you after high school.

College visiting is more an art than a science. Some people have a revelation the moment they set foot on the "right" campus; others keep a methodical checklist to analyze their impressions carefully. The only iron-clad rule is to keep your eyes and ears open—you may not know what you're looking for until it hits you in the face.

PLAN AHEAD

The first step to a successful visit is to make plans early. Since interview schedules at popular schools fill up fast, you should try to call several months ahead of time to make an appointment. (A note to the faint of heart: It's your visit, so *you* should make the call, not your parents.) We recommend that you begin visits in the spring of your junior year and continue them through the summer and fall. Though it's best to visit when classes are in session, many families find that the summer is the only convenient time to visit faraway colleges. A summer visit is better than no visit at all, but keep in mind that the tanned bodies frolicking on the lawns are probably summer-school impostors—maybe even high school students. If you see a campus in the summer that you really like, try to get back to see it while classes are in session before making a final decision.

If you're planning to stay overnight—which you should do if at all possible—ask the admissions office if you can sleep in one of the dorms. During the school year, most colleges will be glad to set you up with a student host. If you want to arrange meetings with professors or coaches, for example, or if there are particular programs that you'd like to learn about in depth, make the arrangements well in advance.

Friday is generally the best day of the week to visit, since you can sample both weekday and weekend activity. Try to avoid exam periods—everyone you meet will be going nuts—and also steer clear of the first week of school in the fall. Though it is natural to want to fit in as many colleges as possible, limit yourself to no more than two per day. Trying to cram in too many, says William Hiss of Bates College, usually results in a student "screaming at Mother or Father to hurry up and find the college when they are lost and five minutes late for the interview." Since the college visit puts your family relationships on public display, avoid like the plague any situation that is likely to create tension between you and your parents.

If you live near the college you are considering, you may have the luxury of visiting more than once. If so, our advice is to go the first time with your parents to get the standard information from the admissions office, and then go again on your own to stay overnight in the dorms and sample student life.

As the visit approaches, do some hard thinking about what is most important to you in a college. Is the quality of the history department really such a big deal to you? Are you dead set on going to a school with a strong Greek system? Do drama facilities still loom as large in your mind as they did six months ago? Once you've settled on some criteria, make a list of the questions you want answered and establish a uniform way of recording your impressions so you can compare different schools on key points.

CUTTING THROUGH THE PROPAGANDA (AGAIN)

On the appointed day, leave early and allow plenty of time to get there, especially if you have any appointments. (See Chapter 14, "Surviving the Interview.") Once you've gotten those out of the way, take a campus tour. It will probably be led by a student, though by no means a typical one. The smiling, affable, oh-so-polite representatives that most colleges recruit as tour guides can lay it on pretty thick. See if your tour guide admits to anything negative; that should give you a good idea of how much of the positive stuff you can believe. Whether or not your guide is completely candid, the tour is valuable because it offers one student's perspective on the college, which you can compare with that of your interviewer or anyone else you happen to meet.

Though listening to the tour guide's monologue is helpful, even more valuable is the chance to engage him or her in conversation. Unfortunately, most high school students seem to develop a sudden case of laryngitis

---

Five Good Questions to Ask Your Tour Guide

Who will teach me? At many universities, senior faculty teach mainly graduate students and upperclassmen. Find out who teaches the general education courses that all students must take during their freshman and sophomore years.

How big are the freshman classes? Forget about student-faculty ratios. Find out how big your classes will be during your first year.

What happens on a typical weekend? This will give you a sense of the overall character of the student body, as well as the range of options that would be open to you as a student.

Do students talk about current issues? Casual conversation says a lot about the intellectual atmosphere of a college. Political and social issues play a key role in student life at some and are hardly ever mentioned at others. Find out if students would rather talk about Bill Clinton or beer bashes.

What are this college's biggest drawbacks? Honest or not, the answer should be interesting.

---

during a campus tour. But why let the pushy mothers have all the fun? Step to the front of the crowd and ask a question! What are the dorms like? Where do people go to have a good time? What are the biggest issues on campus? Don't be afraid to dig beyond the stock answers. If the tour guide boasts about the university's electron microscope, find out if undergraduates get to use it. If the guide says the new gym is state-of-the-art, ask if intramural athletes get the same access as the varsity teams.

There are dozens of questions that you could ask. The box on page 144 gives five we think will be especially revealing.

KEEP YOUR EYES PEELED

In addition to being a good question-and-answer session, the tour will give you a sense for the layout of the campus and the rhythms of a typical day. Keep an eye out for bulletin boards; they will give you a good idea of what is going on. Note the condition of the buildings. Peeling paint and disrepair are signs of a college with financial problems, while new construction is a sign of health. Be sure to ask the guide about any facilities you expected to see if they are not on the route. At the least, the guide can point them out to you on a campus map.

After finishing the standard tour, leave time to roam the campus on your own. This is no time for bashfulness: Corner some students and see if their answers match the ones you got from the tour guide. "Honesty will prevail . . . whether we in admissions like it or not," says Martha Quirk of Principia College.

Obvious places to roam include libraries, classrooms, the dorms, and the student center or central gathering place. See if you can feel the pulse of the campus. Do the students seem friendly? Intellectual? Jocky? Are they radical chic? Or does it feel like you've just stumbled onto the set of *Revenge of the Nerds*?

Sit in on a class, eat a meal in the dining hall, go to a sports event. Are these your kind of people? "I usually tell students to look for the intangibles: friendliness of the students, interaction of faculty and students, excitement in the classroom," says Delsie Phillips of Haverford College. In the end, your gut feeling is probably more important than all the checklists and departmental rankings put together.

Things to Notice on Campus

Buildings in disrepair—the signal of financial problems. One good place to check out: the bathrooms.

New construction—a sign of financial health and a statement of the college's plan for the future.

Seating in the cafeteria: Are students sitting at the same tables with faculty members? Blacks with whites? A good indication of social relationships on campus.

Computers: How up-to-date are the computer labs? How is access to them controlled? Are all dorm rooms wired for computer use? What about access to the Internet?

Size of classrooms: Lots of lecture halls suggest big classes. Lots of seminar rooms means a more personal approach.

Bulletin boards—the single best authority on what students care about.

SAMPLE THE NIGHT LIFE

If you stay in a dorm, your host or hostess will be a gold mine of information. Get him or her to show you around and compare what you see with what you were shown on your official tour. If you're interested in a particular program, ask if he or she can introduce you to a friend who is enrolled in it.

In the evening, relax and hang out with whoever happens to be in the dorm. Apply what Phil Smith of Williams College calls "the 10:30 test." Says he: "Almost all college students get hungry around 10:30 P.M. Between then and midnight tends to be 'people time.' Find out what students are talking about, how they treat one another, the depth of their concerns." Try to stay up for as much of it as you can. Sometimes the most interesting conversations don't really get started until *after* midnight.

As the visit draws to a close, be sure to get your thoughts down on paper while they're still fresh in your mind. Note all the particulars about the academic programs and facilities, but also remember the big picture. Above all, trust your instincts about the people and the place. Can you see yourself as a student? Are these the kind of people you want for friends? Four years is a long time.

14
Surviving the Interview

It is a scene every college applicant dreads: The awkward quiet of an admissions office waiting room, filled with nervous students and parents awaiting the call from within. Mother leans over to straighten your collar as you stare blankly at the pages of a catalogue. The wait seems like an eternity, but finally an admissions officer beckons and ushers you into her office. After a brief exchange of pleasantries, she asks what books you have read lately. "None!" you blurt out. "I hate reading!" With that, you leap to your feet, lift your chair high in the air, and smash it to splinters on top of her desk. As she flees the room in terror, you watch her with a fiendish gleam in your eye, and laugh and laugh and laugh. . . .

Fortunately for those with an active imagination, few applicants actually go berserk in the interview. What's more, the interview isn't nearly as important in the admissions process as most people seem to think.

At many schools, including most large universities, the interview is nothing more than an information session for the benefit of the applicant. Even colleges that use them for admissions purposes realize that twenty minutes of chitchat may not reveal much about the real you—especially if you're nervous. When it does count, the interview almost always works in your favor by putting a human face on your application. As James Holmes of Washington College notes, "It's rare that someone shoots himself in the foot with some horrendous blunder."

Before you hit the panic button about the interview, check with the admissions office to find out their policy. Are the interviews strictly informational, or are they used in making decisions? Many large universities don't even offer campus interviews. Bear in mind that the interview isn't so much a judgment of you as it is one more step in a game of mutual pursuit.

"Treat it as an opportunity to discover whether or not the institution is right for you, not as an obstacle to be overcome," counsels Steven Syverson of Lawrence University. "Remember that the interviewer is usually just as anxious as the student to create a good impression," adds George Stoner of George Washington.

If you're still suffering from those pre-interview jitters, here are some tips for putting your best foot forward:

TRY TO RELAX

On the day of the interview, your first dilemma will be picking what to wear. Be comfortable but dress nicely. You won't need Dad's oversized three-piece suit, but neither should you show up looking like a beach bum. Proper interview attire balances respect for the occasion with the fact that you are a seventeen-year-old.

The first secret to a successful interview is getting there on time. If this is your first visit to the admissions office, leave an extra half hour to get lost on the way. If you do happen to be late, get a grip. Most admissions officers have flexibility in their schedules and won't mind.

The interviewer knows you are going to be nervous, and he or she will almost never hold it against you. Indeed, a little nervousness can actually work in your favor. The fact that you care enough to be nervous will endear you to most interviewers. If you feel the need, say so out loud: "I'm a little nervous, because I really want to come here." Nervousness is bad only when it causes you to clam up—or worse, adopt a posture of cool indifference. When in doubt, be open. Ninety-nine times out of a hundred, the admissions officer will do his or her best to put you at ease.

After the initial pleasantries, there is one major rule to good inter-viewing: have a conversation. Get to know the interviewer, maintain eye contact, and be responsive. Most students come into interviews like robots programmed to talk nonstop for forty-five minutes and then self-destruct. Better to muster the presence of mind to listen and react spontaneously.

TIP *Never schedule your first interview at one of your top-choice schools. Instead, practice your technique at one or two less-desired options before making a date with First Choice U.*

Interviewers come in two basic varieties: talkers and listeners. The talkers are generally more intent on selling their college than on listening to anything you have to say. Don't be frustrated if you have trouble getting a word in edgewise. Affirm what the interviewer says and use openings in the conversation to get your questions answered. If you play the role of interested customer, this sort of interviewer will respond favorably.

The majority of college interviewers are listeners—that is, they view their primary task as getting you to open up about yourself, your ideas, your hopes and dreams. They generally probe for topics that seem to excite passion or interest, while giving you the openings to take the conversation wherever you choose.

We recommend that you go to every interview prepared to discuss at least two or three topics at length. Examples might include your school, your favorite academic subject, important extracurricular activities, current events, or your favorite book. Think carefully about your opinions, how you got them, and what the subject means to you. Many interviewers will use an extended conversation on one subject to measure the depth of your thinking. Be careful not to misrepresent yourself. If you say current events are one of your biggest interests, don't come up blank when the conversation turns to the latest Arab–Israeli peace talks.

No matter who your interviewer is, don't forget to do your homework on the college ahead of time. Well-prepared interviewees should come armed with at least three questions. Good questions, mind you. While an admissions officer is likely to be impressed by a probing question, he is just as likely to be turned off by a stupid one ("Do you have a business department?") that is answered on the first page of the view book. By asking intelligent questions, you let the admissions officer know that you are serious about the matchmaking process. That alone is a big point in your favor.

EXPECT TOUGH QUESTIONS

Though most interviewers will let you take the initiative, don't be surprised if you find yourself on the receiving end of one of these time-honored zingers:

What books have you read lately? Try to avoid the usual high school staples like *Lord of the Flies* or *The Scarlet Letter.* Since part of the purpose is to gauge your initiative and creativity, it is generally best to pick a book you found on your own rather than one that has been assigned. (On the other hand, *The Scarlet Letter* is probably better than *The Michael Jordan Story.*)

Some Good Questions to Ask Your Interviewer

What is distinctive about your school? Try to get beyond the usual platitudes about academic excellence. Each school has a different idea of its mission, which tells you a lot about its character.

What sets students here apart from those at similar schools? If this is Yale, ask about the differences from Harvard or Princeton. You'll probably be considering those competing schools, too, so try to zero in on where each one stands in relation to the others.

What is the retention rate? (What percentage of entering students return for their sophomore year and graduate within five years?) If the rate is low, find out why.

What are your most recent alumni doing? What are the most common career paths? Is this school a feeder for Wall Street, or does everyone want to join the Peace Corps after graduation? Find out whether the aspirations of past graduates match yours.

Would I have been accepted last year? Whether or not you get into a selective college depends mainly on whom you're competing against. Since admissions officers can't predict the exact mix of applicants in any given year, asking about last year makes it easier for them to assess your chances.

Choose a book that really excites you and that you wouldn't mind discussing at length. An in-depth talk about a book you know well will almost always impress an interviewer. By the same token, if you try to wing it, you'll look like a liar and an idiot at the same time.

Why do you want to enroll here? The trick is to cite at least two or three reasons. Read the college's literature and mention what you've found there—diversity, academic excellence, and so on. Mix that with some reasons of your own, like the fact that it is strong in the natural sciences or has good performing-arts facilities. Strike a balance between the things you are interested in and the things the college is trying to sell you on.

What are your most important activities and why are they valuable? Think this out before the interview, and resist the temptation to be too grandiose. Standard answers that cite benefits such as increased self-discipline and experience working with others are fine. If you can think of something more extraordinary—an experience that has transformed your life—so much the better.

What would you add to life at this college? This one is a favorite at highly selective colleges. Hint: List some of the ways that you would affect the lives of others in the community. The purpose of the question is to find out how much you would give of yourself to those around you. Colleges want givers.

What other colleges are you considering? This one is loaded. On the one hand, your list will tell the college something about you and your interests. Your interviewer will know all about the other schools and will be impressed if you can explain your choices cogently. If the list includes colleges that are radically different from one another, explain. Otherwise, it will appear that you haven't done a very good job researching.

On the other hand, the list will give the interviewer an idea of whether his or her college is your first choice—something uppermost in the minds of admissions officers at schools that are usually safeties. If the college is your first choice, stress that fact. If it's your safety, be a little vague. It is always best to give the impression that the college is among your top choices.

KEEP YOUR COOL AND BE YOURSELF

If—God forbid—something does happen, have a sense of humor. This worked for at least one stressed-out applicant to Franklin and Marshall College, who, sitting with her legs crossed, was so nervous that she kept swinging her foot back and forth. It just so happened that she was wearing wooden clogs. On a particularly long swing, the clog flew off, hit the admissions officer in the head, and then ricocheted off his desk lamp, breaking it. "She looked at him in terror, but when their glances met, they both dissolved in laughter," recalls Ronald Potier. No big deal.

The interview is also a good time to introduce ticklish subjects head on. Too many applicants try to paper over problems because they think colleges are looking for perfect applicants. In reality, college interviewers tend to be impressed by students who are mature enough to be candid about the

Post-Interview Stress Syndrome

One applicant to Haverford College was particularly stressed out at the conclusion of his interview. On his way back to the waiting room, he opened a series of doors. Upon reaching the waiting room, he was too nervous to notice and instead opened one more door—and walked into a closet. He was so embarrassed that he simply stayed there. "It was some minutes before he came out to face the room full of people staring at him," recalls Delsie Phillips of Haverford admissions.

obstacles they have overcome. The worst thing you can do is to leave a dip in performance unexplained. If, for instance, you had a poor sophomore year because of switching to a new school, the interview is an excellent time to tell your story. If you have a learning disability that has meant lower grades in certain subjects, say so and then explain the steps you have taken to compensate and how you plan to cope in college.

In cases like these, applicants should consider bringing a transcript to show what they are talking about. A transcript can also be useful if you are particularly interested in an assessment of your admission chances. In most other situations, a transcript is not necessary. The whole purpose of the interview is to reveal things *not* included in all the paper that will accompany your application.

Though parents can be very helpful on a college visit, make sure they *do not* venture into the interview room. Though they mean well, parents can do nothing to help the situation—and plenty to mess it up. They're generally more nervous than you are, and they tend to babble. Suggest that they take a tour or get lunch while you're in the interview. If they want to come back at the end for a question or two in the waiting room, that's perfectly okay (but only after you've had your thirty minutes alone with the admissions officer). Above all, don't have a family squabble in the presence of your interviewer. Even if you roll your eyes at something your mom says, you are broadcasting your immaturity for everyone to see. If she says the stupidest thing you've ever heard (a strong possibility), just keep your cool.

When D-Day arrives, resist the temptation to try too hard. This is no time to create an artificial personality or "market" yourself as something you're not. "Sometimes applicants are obviously coached," cautions

Delsie Phillips of Haverford. "Their 'image' is overplayed, and it looks and feels uncomfortable." Nothing is more irritating than a seventeen-year-old who acts as if he or she has all the answers. Though preparation is important, the golden rule for good interviewing is really quite simple: Be yourself.

15
Getting Good Recommendations

There is a rule of thumb among admissions officers: "The thicker the file, the thicker the kid."

What that means, in practical terms, is that if you're thinking of padding your application with a few recommendations from well-placed friends of the family, forget it. "Each year we run an informal contest to determine the candidate with the most superfluous recommendations," reports Robert Jones of Hampden-Sydney College. "This year's winner had twenty-three, and he was denied."

Don't misunderstand. Recommendations can be useful, but only if they come from people who know you well. A good one will tell the admissions committee something about you as a person that comes out nowhere else in the application—your willingness to work hard, perhaps, or your ability to listen to good advice and then use it. Recommendations that begin with phrases like "I don't know Susie personally, but if she is anything like her parents . . ." are a cinch to start eyes rolling.

ACCENT ON ACADEMICS

To get good recommendations, find people who are familiar with your goals and aspirations and can write about you in vivid detail. (You usually won't be able to look at the recommendations before they're sent, so choose carefully.) Most selective colleges require at least one recommendation from a teacher. Since colleges want to know what you have done lately, try to pick teachers who have taught you in your junior or senior year.

English teachers tend to write well, so they are usually a good bet. To

Your Rights Under the Buckley Amendment

You might not know it, but because of an act of Congress you have the right to look at your recommendations *after* they are filed at the colleges. The issue is complex (dealing with the limits of your right to privacy), but the upshot is this: Most recommendation forms have a place to check off if you want to sign away your rights under the Buckley Amendment. Though a lawyer might tell you never to sign away your rights, we think you should in this instance. Signing the waiver is an expression of confidence in your recommenders, who may feel freer to be candid. Most important, the colleges will be reassured that you are not worried about what your recommenders might say.

round out the picture, consider a second recommender in math, science, or a foreign language. An academic teacher who has also known you outside the classroom is generally the best choice, but try to avoid coaches or teachers of fluffy electives. Even if you are pals with the yearbook sponsor, your math teacher is likely to have more clout with an admissions office.

In general, it is best to pick a teacher who respects you as a person and who can testify to some of your deeper and less obvious qualities. It is *not* always best to pick the teacher who gave you the highest grade. Says Tim Fuller of Houghton College, "If a student has cruised through a class and gotten an A, a recommendation from that teacher concerning his or her natural abilities may not be as helpful to the student's admission chances as one where the student has had to struggle and work hard to get a B."

GUIDANCE: HANDLE WITH CARE

Many colleges require a recommendation from the guidance office. The usefulness of this recommendation will hinge on how much firsthand information about you the counselor has.

At a small high school, the counselor often knows everyone and can provide a good overview of your academic career based on his or her knowledge and on input from a number of teachers. At larger ones, there's little chance of that happening unless you're an academic superstar. The only way the counselor will know firsthand of your work is if you keep him or her up to date.

In either case, it is a good idea to establish a personal relationship with the counselor to avoid a recommendation confined to meaningless generalities. (See Chapter 4, "Getting a Jump Start.") Otherwise, you run the risk of suffering a fate similar to that of the luckless applicant to St. John's College in New Mexico who had a recommendation that stated simply, "Joe is really amazing. He does things that are just not normal."

Having chosen your recommenders, don't be bashful. Responsible teachers will rarely say no, but if they hint that someone else might be better, by all means heed their advice.

Popular teachers tend to be snowed under with requests by December, so try to get to them early to make the process as painless as possible. If a teacher expresses uncertainty about how to write a recommendation, photocopy this chapter and give it to him or her. In any case make the process painless for your teacher. (You may be the 20th student who has asked.) Be sure to fill out the top portion and provide a stamped envelope addressed to the admissions office. Just as important, provide a brief synopsis of your goals, interests, and the experiences you have shared with the teacher on a separate piece of paper. That will help the teacher focus his or her thoughts and increase the likelihood that the teacher's comments will reinforce the other points you are trying to make in your application.

HOW THICK IS TOO THICK?

Occasionally, students may want to send along an extra recommendation beyond those requested in the application. Though the first impulse should always be to send the one or two best recommendations, an extra one from someone who knows you well may not hurt, especially if the extra recommender can highlight a different facet of your record or personality than the others. As a rule, you should not exceed the number of recommendations requested by more than one. (The wait list is an exception to this rule. See Chapter 20, "Fat Letters and Thin.")

Notwithstanding what we said about friends in high places, some applicants will want to see if their family connections can come through in a pinch. If you are a relative or close family friend of someone who gave millions to the college, that may help. If your best friend's Dad is an alumnus, have him write a letter, but don't get your hopes up. A recommendation from someone who knows you a little or not at all—from your local congressman to the president of the United States—is probably worthless. Scattershot attempts at influence peddling will only succeed in making you look silly.

Consider the examples brought to us by former Virginia Military Institute Admissions Dean William J. Buchanan: "We had an alumnus solicit letters of recommendation for his son from his 200+ VMI classmates. No dice. . . . One applicant (over 1400 SAT) sent letters of recommendation from an archbishop, an illiterate scoutmaster, and a man identifying himself as a former captain in the czar's Imperial Guard. No sale again. (This lad got A's in courses he liked and F's in those he didn't.)" The reason these examples were no good? No personal insights.

On the other hand, sometimes it pays to consider a slightly offbeat approach. One possibility is a peer reference from one of your classmates who knows you well and is a good writer. (This type of recommendation is required at Williams College.) Michael Behnke of MIT was much impressed by a letter from a school custodian about how hard an applicant worked with the custodial staff on school projects: "In broken English, the custodian communicated very effectively that this applicant was the only student in the school who paid attention to those who worked in support positions." That sort of recommendation is generally a lot more valuable than one from even the biggest bigwig.

16
The Right Way to Fill Out Your Applications

Sometimes college applicants defy all logic. They agonize for months over taking the SAT, fork over hundreds of dollars for application fees, and travel far and wide to visit colleges. But when it comes time to fill out the applications, they dash them off in an hour or two without even bothering to proofread.

Or so it seems. How else do you explain the thousands of applications every year—many from excellent students—that are positively riddled with typos, spelling mistakes, correction fluid, and barely legible scribbles in the margins? "A sloppy application is the quickest way to take yourself out of the running at a highly selective college," declares Richard Steele of Bowdoin College. Whether you file your application via computer disk or use the traditional paper variety, remember that the application is *you* in the eyes of the admissions office. Here are a few bite-size morsels on how to do the job right:

BE NEAT

If you plan to file the paper application, make at least two photocopies of the original. You can practice on them and get all the typos and tomato sauce stains out of your system. Before laying a finger on the original form, proofread the final rough draft for spelling, spacing, word choice, and anything else you can think of. Type the final copy yourself, if at all possible, and don't worry about a few neatly corrected errors. A trace of correction fluid here and there is proof that a high school student actually filled it out—as opposed to Mom or Dad's secretary. If typing presents a major challenge, neatly handwritten responses are acceptable for the fill-in-the-blank portions. But any question that requires more than a sentence should be typed or done on a computer and then inserted with a careful cut-and-paste job.

COMPUTER CONVENIENCE

More and more applicants are using technology to bypass the headaches of paper applications. Many colleges produce applications on disk, and growing numbers are making them available for downloading from their World Wide Web sites. A number of private outfits also make disk copies of applications available, usually for a fee, and many high school guidance offices now have access to electronic applications through a College Board software program. (For more information, see your guidance counselor.) Use of the computer options won't help or hurt your chances. The issue is purely convenience.

Disk or no, all applications are still converted to paper for evaluation. Don't be content with proofing what you see on your computer screen; make a printout to examine what the admissions officer will actually be looking at when the file is printed. The computer can help you cut down on mistakes, but it can also create new ones if you don't proofread with care. Lastly, don't forget to sign the form, a critical detail overlooked by many disk filers.

THE COMMON APPLICATION

Another time saver is the Common Application, available from your guidance office on paper or on disk (or via the World Wide Web—see "Where to Learn More"). Approximately 150 colleges, including most highly selective liberal arts colleges, will accept the Common Application in lieu of their own. Simply fill it out and send photocopies to each participating college. (Be aware that some colleges require supplementary material.)

By endorsing the Common Application, colleges vouch for the fact that it carries the same weight as their own application. Nevertheless, many applicants are leery of it, believing (subconsciously, at least) that colleges will favor applicants who use the college's application. Our solution? Apply to your first choice college(s) with their forms. For additional colleges, feel free to use the Common.

How Many Colleges Should I Apply To?

A good ballpark figure is six, including approximately two from each of the following three categories: (1) reach schools, (2) 50/50 schools, (3) safe schools. The purpose is to apply to colleges of varying degrees of selectivity in order to maximize chances for success.

Most students have no trouble finding the reaches. These are the dream schools, where the odds of admission are long. There is nothing wrong with dreaming, but it also pays to include one or two where the odds are closer to 50/50. Last but not least, applicants should find at least one or two colleges where they would be happy to attend and are reasonably certain of admission.

Though applicants tend to focus more on the reaches, careful selection of the safe ones is probably more important. Getting caught without a school is the ultimate nightmare, almost as bad as attending a poorly chosen safety that doesn't meet your needs.

Some applicants react to runaway college anxiety by applying to a dozen or more schools. We counsel against such a scattershot approach. Confusion and overload are usually the result. Even if you are admitted to ten schools, you can still only attend one. The time to narrow your choices is before you apply, not after.

USE YOUR HEAD

When the application asks for a Visa number, don't fill in the one from Dad's credit card. The question is for foreigners, a fact that will be clear if you read it carefully. Also, don't answer with strained attempts at humor. One admissions director cited with disgust the applicant who listed one of his favorite activities as "beating my grandmother with a tire iron." Ugh! The short-answer questions are not the place to be funny.

If Mom and Dad's "fingerprints" show up on the application anywhere—for example, if it has two different kinds of handwriting—you've got a credibility problem. Get them to proofread and make suggestions if you like, but do the final draft yourself.

CHOOSING A MAJOR

At highly selective schools, even little things like your expected major can have strategic significance. Many universities have different admissions standards across their various colleges and schools. At Georgetown, the acceptance rate is less than 20 percent in the Liberal Arts and Sciences but more than 40 percent in the Faculty of Languages and Linguistics and over 60 percent in the School of Nursing. At virtually any college, the more people who want to major in your chosen field, the harder it is to get in. Premed and engineering are notoriously difficult across the board. Other fields vary, depending on the strength of the college's reputation in that particular area (for example, Bard College, a magnet for artists, is much easier to get into for aspiring physicists).

Applicants should be careful not to misrepresent themselves on the application, but they should also think twice before listing a popular major as their first choice. If you are merely *considering* pre-med, you should probably list "undecided" for your major, a perfectly respectable choice for anyone.

LISTING ACTIVITIES

First rule: Always list activities from most important to least important. The ones that are significant, as evidenced by leadership and time commitment, will be obvious. Marginal stuff like membership in SADD or Monogram Club for varsity athletes should be deemphasized. Don't make a big production out of "honors" from companies that put your picture in a book and then ask you to buy it; such things carry little weight.

Follow the college's preferred format for listing activities. Since the space on the application is often absurdly small, attach extra sheets where necessary. Some applicants prepare their own résumés or activity sheets. Those are often useful as supplemental material, especially when activities of in-depth involvement need further elaboration. But submit one of these only in addition to filling out the college's activity form. When slogging through a pile of a hundred applications, admissions officers prefer to find information in the familiar place and in the standard format rather than finding the words "see attached."

TIP

Never *mail an application without keeping a photo-copy. The number that gets lost is tiny, but you never know.*

EXPLAIN EVERYTHING

Sometimes there is no alternative to attaching extra sheets. If one of your important activities was chairing the Founder's Day Committee, it won't mean anything to the admissions office unless you explain what you did and why the committee was important. If it was an honor bestowed on only one senior, say so. If it involved presentations to alumni and coordination of twenty volunteers for six months, spell that out. Or have the principal write a letter outlining the significance.

The same applies to less pleasant subjects. If there is a black mark on your record—like a suspension or a failing grade—don't just hope that the admissions office won't notice. Any reasonable explanation you can give without sounding whiny or bitter would be helpful. (Even more impressive would be an account of how the experience has helped you to mature.)

APPLICATION EXTRAS

Some students may be tempted to send along some extra material to supplement the application. If you are an athlete or a musician, you may want to consider making a tape of your performance(s). For artists, a portfolio of work can be useful, even if you are not applying to an art program. Don't be too shy to send extra exhibits, but only if they show genuine distinction. Just because your mother was enthralled by your recent chorus solo doesn't mean you should send the tape. The music expert on the admissions committee—who has probably received a thousand such tapes—may not be so impressed.

Before sending extra material, we recommend that you call the admissions office to ask for advice. Some prefer that you forward it directly to a particular person; others request that supplements fit in an 8-by-11-inch file folder. If you are an athlete, such material should almost always go to the coach.

GIMMICKS

As "getting-in mania" sweeps the nation each spring, eager applicants shower admissions offices with everything from cookies and flowers to letters with various creative ways of saying "Please accept me!" We recommend that you refrain from acts of desperation like these. The tricks have all been tried before.

We don't mean to discourage real creativity, such as that shown by the applicant who wrote to the admissions office as if he were a wealthy donor preparing to make a contribution. Only in a postscript did he disclose that he was really a freshman applicant demonstrating what he could do in ten years if admitted. (He was.) There is a big difference between this interesting twist and the vacuous attention-getting moves described above.

GET IT IN EARLY

Keep on top of those deadlines. Most come between January and April, but a handful of state universities make priority deadlines as early as October. Find out if your colleges offer rolling admissions (many state schools do) or if they evaluate applications in one big pool. Under rolling admissions, colleges admit the first good applicants who come down the pike, adding to the urgency of prompt filing. At most other colleges, filing by the deadline ensures full consideration, but mailing the application early is a good idea. A tidal wave of applications pours in as the deadline approaches, and the ones caught in that last-minute surge sometimes get less attention.

Most applicants heave a sigh of relief when they mail the application, but the job is still not finished. As the deadline approaches, be sure to pay a friendly follow-up call on your recommenders. Approximately two weeks after everything has been sent, call the admissions offices to verify that your application is complete. If a stray recommendation still has not arrived, don't fret. Calmly inquire with the teacher, and rest assured that the colleges will not hold it against you.

When the last application is safely tucked away in the admissions-office folder, your part of the job is done. Take time to kick back. You deserve it!

17
Scoring Points with the Essay

Pity the poor admissions officer, sitting alone in his cramped little office, swamped by a stack of essays six inches thick. Talk about an endurance test!

"How My Trip to Europe Changed My Life"

"How I Would Solve World Hunger"

"Why I Want to Be an Investment Banker"

The problem with these essays? No personality. They're written by applicants who don't have a clue how to choose a topic that will reveal something meaningful about themselves. The result is a generic, contrived, fake essay that will bore the socks off even the most conscientious admissions officer.

Your essay will eventually find its way into the same pile as these, so why not try to shake the admissions officer out of his stupor? Let him have a peek inside your world, and at the same time show him how well you can write and think. He is interested in learning about you or he would not be in admissions.

THE WRITE STUFF

What do admissions officers want in an essay? "Spark, vitality, wit, sensitivity, originality, and signs of a lively mind" are some of the qualities, according to Richard Steele of Bowdoin. First and foremost, they want to know how well you express yourself in writing. The sad fact is, many high

165

school students can't write well, and unfortunately, this book can't teach you how. If you doubt your skills, talk it over with your English teacher or get help from your parents or a tutor. (Two good books on the subject are *The Elements of Style,* by William Strunk and E. B. White, and *On Writing Well,* by William Zinsser.)

In the meantime, try to be as concise and specific as possible. Carefully organize your essay around a key theme. Don't waste words that aren't essential to your point, and reread the essay several times for word choice and typos. Above all, *use your spell checker.*

If you have the time, put your essay aside for a week or two and then

Five Fundamentals of a Successful Essay

Show, don't tell. If you want to convince the reader that you never give up, don't tell the reader, "I never give up." Instead, describe how you were cut from the basketball team in ninth grade, sat on the bench in tenth grade, and finally made the team as a junior. A skillful writer lets evidence *show* that a proposition is true; a clumsy one *tells,* because his writing is not powerful enough to show.

Use your own experiences. The most interesting essay puts you in the starring role and features real life thoughts and feelings. Anecdotes from your world are always more interesting than abstractions. Give the reader a piece of your mind.

Use the first person. The fact that it is a "personal" essay provides a strong hint. Nine out of ten essays should be in the first person, the best vehicle for revealing your thoughts and beliefs.

Begin with a flourish. The most important sentence in any essay is the first one. Polish it like a precious stone. Good writers often try to hook the reader with a first sentence that surprises, piques, or begins an interesting story.

Proofread. Applicants are told over and over again, and still they don't proofread! Arrggh! Nothing is more damaging than an essay full of typos, misspellings, and grammatical mistakes.

read it again to see if it still makes sense. You'll be amazed at how many mistakes jump out that were invisible the first time. By choosing your words carefully and proofreading, you show the admissions office not only that you are a good writer but also that you care about the essay and are willing to take the time to do it right.

STRAIGHT FROM THE HEART

Though all the technical advice is important, you don't have to be another Joyce Carol Oates to write a good essay. Most admissions offices won't penalize you if there are a few rough edges to it—unless you happen to be applying to places like Princeton or Swarthmore.

Aside from writing skills, the most important thing admissions officers look for in the essay is a sense of who you are as a person. "We look for the applicant's voice," says one. It is generally easier to reveal something about yourself if you pick a topic drawn from your own experiences. Write about your unique perspective on something—a relationship, perhaps—or explain an incident that helped you learn an important lesson. Putting the experience on paper is usually the easy part; more challenging is how to write about what it means. Too many applicants feel they must make a single experience bear the burden of transforming their lives. Nine times out of ten, the "How _____ Changed My Life" essay falls flat. Few teenagers have actually had such experiences, a fact admissions people know all too well. A more believable approach is to write thoughtfully about incremental change, with a particular incident used to illustrate your evolution.

The best topics are often close to the heart. If you have the guts to openly discuss a personal problem or obstacle you have overcome, any admissions officer will be impressed. A good essay always shares something real, even though baring your soul to complete strangers may feel uncomfortable. One University of Tulsa applicant scored major points with an essay about looking in the mirror and reflecting on his homely face. An applicant to Lewis and Clark College turned the tables by writing as if she were an admissions officer considering her own application. A Rollins College hopeful enhanced his chances with an essay on his guilt over injuring another player in a football game, while a Duke applicant scored major points with a spoof on the anxiety related to taking the SAT.

One applicant to Hampden-Sydney College wrote about a pair of old but treasured shoes he had worn to his interview despite his mother's protests, ending with, "Tell the truth, Dean Jones, did you notice my shoes?"

"My response was yes, but it didn't matter," says Robert Jones, who offered him admission.

DON'T TRY TO SAVE THE WORLD

While personal topics work well, stay away from political issues or what one admissions officer calls the "social-problem-of-the-year" bandwagon.

The bandwagon works like this: Suppose there is a huge oil spill next year in the Gulf of Mexico. Like clockwork, college applicants across the nation will start writing essays on the environment and why we need to keep it clean. Most of them will say the same thing, more or less, and even the well-written ones will reveal little about the writer and his or her outlook on life.

Essays that are overly self-centered also bomb. "I hated it when an applicant wrote that he had learned from a trip to the ghetto how fortunate he is to live in a nice house," says Richard Wood of Colorado College. A societal problem can occasionally be an interesting topic for an essay, but only if you give it a personal slant. Lots of people write about the homeless, usually a mistake. But one applicant to the University of Miami actually went out and interviewed a homeless man—and was accepted.

In addition to open-ended personal statements, many applications ask students to answer a more specific essay question. Sooner or later, you will probably be asked to:

- reflect on an experience that has had a profound impact on your life
- discuss the extracurricular activity that was most important to you and why
- write page 199 of your autobiography

The most important rule of thumb in cases like these is simple: *Answer the question.* Never substitute the answer to one college's question for that of another unless the two are exactly the same.

Another morsel: If you're doing all your essays on a word processor, remember to change the name of the college before you print. Likewise, heed the advice of Roger Campbell of the University of Denver: "Don't send a Xerox copy of your most recent major school paper. We may not agree with your teacher."

Essay Turnoffs

- **Trite phrases.** Most admissions officers are near nausea with applicants who "want to help people." Think of something that is unique about you.
- **Slickness.** An essay that reads as if it has been churned out by Dad's public-relations firm will not impress. Let the real you shine through.
- **Cynicism.** Colleges want bright, active people—not wet blankets. A positive approach to life, and to the essay, will score points.
- **Life histories.** Make sure your essay has a point. An endless stream of phrases like "then I did this, and then I did this" is sleep-inducing and doesn't say anything meaningful.
- **Essay that goes on forever.** More is not better. The colleges want a concise, well-reasoned essay—not the sequel to *War and Peace*. Try not to exceed the amount of space allotted for each essay.
- **The thesaurus syndrome.** Don't overutilize ostentatiously pretentious language to delineate the thematic observations you are endeavoring to articulate. Big words aren't impressive; a clear, direct style is.

IS LAUGHTER THE BEST MEDICINE?

An obvious way to make yourself memorable is to use a little humor. Many admissions officers enjoy essays written with a twinkle in the eye. An applicant to Ursinus College made a lasting impression when he wrote his essay on, ahem, sexual fantasies. (He was accepted.)

Be on guard, though, because humor is in the eye of the beholder, and it's hard to be sure the admissions staff will laugh when you want them to. Also, "It usually makes the student seem too casual, too uninterested, and/or flippant," says Richard Hallin of Eckerd College. Only excellent writers should try to be funny, and then only if they can reveal something important about themselves in the process.

As for length, we wholeheartedly recommend the KISS formula of Tim Fuller of Houghton (Keep It Short and Simple). Admissions officers reading "their seven hundredth application in two weeks," he says, "are not impressed by long essays."

A final ticklish issue is getting help. There's a fine line between legitimate consultation and illegitimate misrepresentation. The application has your name on it, so most of it should be your work. It's fine to get a parent or teacher to look it over for spelling and make some comments on style and content, but if that person begins writing sentences or paragraphs, it isn't your essay anymore. Many admissions officers have finely honed radar to detect ghostwritten essays. If you got straight B's in English and your essay reads like E. B. White, the admissions office is going to be skeptical.

"Essays are windows into the real you," says David Erdmann of Rollins College. After completing a rough draft, ask yourself: Could anybody else have written this essay? If so, you need to think again about the fine art of letting the reader see inside your soul.

PART THREE

PAYING THE BILL

18
The New Financial Aid Game

If David Letterman ever compiled a Top Ten List of the most boring subjects on the planet, college financial aid would rank near the top. Even the most conscientious applicant will probably begin to feel his or her eyelids getting heavy after just a few minutes of contemplating Expected Family Contributions (EFCs), Student Aid Reports (SARs), and the Free Application for Federal Student Aid (FAFSA). But unless your last name happens to be Rockefeller or Gates, you had better wake up and listen closely. In today's college admissions, financial aid is a make-or-break proposition. The path to First Choice U. is littered with applicants who realized too late that getting financial aid can be just as important as getting in.

For anyone planning to let dear old Mom and Dad foot the bill, here are some sobering facts:

- The cost of attending the most prestigious private colleges for four years is now approximately $125,000, more than double the price in the early 1980s.
- Tuition at public universities is rising just as fast—up 76 percent in the past ten years, according to the College Board.
- While college costs have gone through the roof, government aid has failed to keep pace. Many programs have been slashed; others have disappeared entirely.

For families that don't have an extra $100,000 stashed under the mattress, money will influence the college search at every step. The schools don't like to say so in public, but many are forced to admit and deny students according to financial criteria. We'll tell you when it happens and to whom. Colleges are also less and less likely to provide all the financial aid that applicants need to enroll. We'll show you the causes of the money shortage and the colleges' fancy dancing to cover it up. Today's financial-aid scene is more complicated—and more deceptive—than ever before. While colleges charge sticker prices in excess of $25,000 for a single year, they also offer an elaborate network of discounts based on need and merit. We'll tell you where the hidden money is and how to maximize your chances of getting some.

We begin with a few pointers about the financial-aid search and an overview of how the system is supposed to work—and *did* work once upon a time. The basic ground rules haven't changed much in a generation. The difference is how the colleges manipulate and use the results. After covering the fundamentals, we tackle the nitty-gritty of how financial aid works today.

FINANCIAL AID 101

The first rule of financial aid is simple: The colleges are the place to find it. About 95 percent of the available dollars are administered through them, including all of the federal money. We'll suggest other places to look later on, but this chapter focuses solely on college-administered aid.

As we have noted, college-administered financial aid comes in two basic varieties: awards based on academic merit or special talents, and awards based on need. Your first major decision in the financial-aid search is whether or not to apply for need-based aid. In most cases, the answer should be yes. Even if your family income is over $100,000, there is still a chance that you may qualify for something. We recommend that you sit down with your parents at the outset of the college search and ask a simple question: How much can the family afford to pay each year for college? A ballpark figure will do. Next, compare that number with the total of tuition, room and board, and fees (plus $2,000 for travel, books, and living expenses) at the college(s) you are interested in attending. If the total of those is larger than what your parents feel they can afford, you should definitely apply for financial aid.

The talk with your parents should inject a dose of reality into your college search. If the figure they can pay is below the cost of your schools, you need to investigate some cheaper options. But don't eliminate the expensive ones just yet. Apply for aid and see what you can get. The time to judge whether a college is too expensive comes at the end of the process, after the financial-aid awards have been made. Only then will you know the actual out-of-pocket costs of each school.

To illustrate this point, we offer the following example. Let's assume that a close personal friend of yours named Todd Tight-Wad is applying to two schools: an expensive private college charging $25,000 per year and a state university with a more modest sticker price of $10,000. Which one do you think will end up costing Todd's family more? The one that costs $25,000, right? Maybe—but maybe not.

When Todd applies for financial aid, the system reviews his family's assets and calculates something called the Expected Family Contribution (EFC)—the amount Todd's family can afford for college. Let's say his family's EFC is $7,000. If the colleges are willing and able, they'll give Todd financial aid to cover his "demonstrated need"—the difference between the EFC and their sticker price. At the expensive private college, he would qualify for $18,000 in aid, while at the public university he would get only $3,000. Even though the sticker prices of the two are vastly different, they both end up costing him $7,000. Even if his EFC were much higher—$15,000 or so—he would still qualify for $10,000 from the private college to help soften the blow. In a few cases, the expensive college might actually turn out to be cheaper. Public universities are typically much less generous with need-based aid than private ones, and if the private one meets Todd's full demonstrated need while the public one meets none of it, the pricey $25,000 private school turns out to be $3,000 cheaper when all is said and done.

For an early indication of how the system might work for your family, we recommend that you complete one of the financial aid estimators that are available via the World Wide Web (and from many financial aid offices on paper and/or disk). These programs replicate the aid formulas used to calculate need. Simply plug in your family's financial data, and voilà—out comes the EFC. For convenience and reliability, we recommend the College Board's aid estimator on its Web site at www.collegeboard.com.

If you and your parents are careful with your data, the estimator should give a rough idea of how much aid you can expect. The results will help dictate your financial aid strategy. If your EFC is over $25,000, your best hope of aid probably lies in merit scholarships (described on page 177). If your EFC is less than $10,000, you'll want to look at schools with a firm commitment to need-based aid.

We emphasize that an aid estimator will give only a *rough* idea of your possible award. With college purse strings pulled tighter every year, the financial-aid system is less reliable than ever before. Families can no longer sit back and trust that they'll get all the money they need. One essential strategy is to apply to one or more schools where you are sure your family can pay the sticker price. Second, you and your parents should do a thorough job of financial aid comparison shopping before you apply. The new world of financial aid has more twists and turns than a Stephen King thriller. The time has come to move beyond Financial Aid 101.

THE BUDGET SQUEEZE HITS HIGHER ED

To understand the plight of the financial aid system in the late 1990s, you need a brief history lesson. The roots of today's crisis go back to the 1960s and the glory days of the civil rights movement. The federal government had declared a "War on Poverty," and the colleges were determined to take the lead in breaking down the walls of oppression. College admissions offices made a commitment to admit students without regard for their ability to pay and to then cover the full financial need of any who chose to enroll. Though the most generous support was offered to low-income applicants, affluent families also reaped handsome rewards; even millionaires could qualify for interest-free loans subsidized and guaranteed by the government. No matter what your background or financial circumstances, aid was available for the asking.

Somewhere on the road to utopia, financial reality intruded and the high-minded ideal of need-based aid was compromised. The country took a turn toward conservatism in the 1980s, and government spending suddenly went from being considered a noble social cause to being viewed as an excuse to raise taxes. In the new political climate, it was only a matter of time before college financial aid went on the chopping block. The states were the first to go for the jugular, slashing millions in aid to public universities, beginning in the late 1980s. The changes in federal money were slower but relentless. Although the total amount of federal assistance is now at an all-time high, the nature of this aid has changed dramatically. The proportion coming in the form of outright grants has declined, while the number and dollar volume of repayable loans has increased. Among loans, there has been a major shift from subsidized loans, under which the government pays the interest while the student is in college, to ones carrying no subsidies.

As government support waned, expenses were rising steeply at the nation's colleges and universities. The cost of physical plant, maintenance, technology, libraries, faculty salaries, and benefits all rose faster than inflation throughout the 1980s. Yet many colleges put off the day of reckoning, preferring to raise tuition rather than deal with the underlying problems. Oddly, the public played along with the game for many years. Since the Ivy League led the way with huge tuition increases, high price seemed to equal high quality.

In the early 1990s, the colleges suddenly awoke to the fact that many families could no longer afford their product. As the money squeeze intensified, the old financial-aid system quickly became unworkable. Most private colleges and many public ones have adopted a rebate system worthy of a used car lot. Though the "sticker price" may be outrageously high, they offer an endless variety of incentive deals and give-backs to lighten the load. (At one selective university in the northeast, not a single freshman paid full tuition and fees in a recent year.) "The admissions process we knew ten years ago is radically different," says Thomas Anthony, former dean of admissions at Colgate University. "Today is much more sales-oriented, and financial aid is now a tool to help colleges in a competitive marketplace."

MERIT SCHOLARSHIPS

The typical private college hands out tens of millions of dollars in financial aid each year. Ask a college administrator why colleges spend so much and you'll probably hear the familiar 1960s-style platitudes about helping the needy, access for all, the value of diversity, and so on. In fact, financial aid has become Weapon #1 in the dog-eat-dog competition for academic prestige and financial stability. Not only do colleges use aid money to lure top students, they also use it as a way to attract paying customers. Strange as it may seem, colleges have figured out that they can make money by giving it away.

The newest gun in the financial aid arsenal—merit scholarships—has been growing by leaps and bounds. Once upon a time, selective colleges looked down their noses at the very idea of "buying" students with merit scholarships. Not only were such awards viewed as undignified, they put a serious crimp in the system of need-based aid for all. The more heavily a college invests in merit scholarships, the less money it has for packages

TIP The growth of merit scholarships carries a clear message: Work hard in school. A few extra points on your GPA could mean thousands of extra dollars in aid.

based on need. Since the students who win merit awards (particularly those based on SAT scores) tend to come from well-heeled families, merit scholarships represent a huge money transfer away from high-need applicants toward low-need ones.

From the colleges' point of view, merit money has become a case of keeping up with the Joneses. As their competitors entice top applicants with lucrative awards, few colleges can afford to sit out the bidding war. Only a handful of the most prestigious—with their massive resources and sterling reputations—continue to offer financial aid solely on the basis of need. These richer colleges have a secret weapon: Because they are so prominent, they tend to attract richer applicants. Thus, at ultra-elite Amherst College, only about 40 percent of the students receive aid from the college, well below the 75 percent that is typical at less-selective private colleges. With more tuition money flowing in from the full payers, Amherst can afford to give aid only on the basis of need.

Colleges that are lower on the prestige totem pole have no such luxury. They resort to merit scholarships to raise their status in the rankings and protect their turf against competitors. Much of the loot goes to top scholars and athletes, with lesser amounts set aside for those with other special talents. Though many schools combine a handful of merit scholarships with abundant need-based aid, those that trumpet dozens of merit scholarships are sending two messages: (1) If you are a well-qualified applicant without much need, a scholarship could be yours. (2) If you are a middle- to high-need student, you might want to look at schools with a firmer commitment to need-based aid.

For applicants who are in earnest about finding a merit scholarship, we offer an ironclad rule: The higher you rank in a particular college's applicant pool, the more likely it is that you will qualify for a merit scholarship. For example, picture applicant Sarah Superstar, with 1400 SATs and a 3.7 grade point average. Sarah is applying to only two schools: Top-of-the-Heap University and Up-and-Coming College. At Top-of-the-Heap, Sarah is well qualified for admission but doesn't stand out from hundreds of other superstars with similar records. But at Up-and-Coming, Sarah is one of the best applicants of the year and considered a hot prospect for the honors program.

Let's assume that Sarah gets in at both schools. Where do you think she will enroll? Nine times out of ten, Sarah and the other superstars will want to go to Top-of-the-Heap. So how does Up-and-Coming compete? By offering Sarah a $20,000 merit scholarship and thereby putting her in a dilemma. Does she pay through the nose to attend the college she really wants? Or does she take the money and attend the less-selective school? Only Sarah and her parents can make that decision.

In addition to the full-tuition scholarship that Sarah won, a second variety of "merit" awards—known to insiders as "discounts"—is now in vogue at many financial-aid offices. Discounts come in the form of small cash awards, usually in the $5,000 range. Though colleges dress them up like big merit awards—same flattering letter, same fancy stationery—the real purpose is to attract affluent students who can pay most of the tuition bill. (People are more likely to respond if they believe they have won something—just ask the folks at Publisher's Clearing House.) In the same way that automakers give factory rebates when they have trouble selling cars at the full price, colleges offer discounts when they have trouble attracting enough full-paying customers. In the late 1990s, the list of schools offering discounts includes most of the expensive private colleges in the nation.

The financial rewards of discounting can be substantial. Consider the situation of Almost Ivy U., a well-known Midwestern liberal arts school that is struggling with financial difficulties and a declining enrollment. Let's assume that Almost Ivy is trying to decide what to do with a $25,000 piece of its financial-aid budget. In past years, it might have lavished the whole amount on an applicant like Monica, who grew up in a housing project and can't afford a dime for college expenses. Monica is likely to be a sentimental favorite of the admissions committee, but with the university's financial security at stake, Almost Ivy simply can't afford her. Instead, the university has earmarked the $25,000 to try to lure a few more students who can pay most or all of the freight. The beneficiaries are Susan, Joe, Michael, Becky, and Jim, five suburban kids who all come from reasonably affluent backgrounds. All five are better-than-average students, but they wouldn't have been merit-scholarship material without their significant financial resources. Each will get a $5,000 "merit" award as the equivalent of a cash incentive to enroll.

The rationale behind Almost Ivy's decision will be clear from a glance at the table on page 180. Were Monica to receive the money, her EFC of $0 would leave the university with nothing to offset its four-year expenditure of $100,000 except the warm fuzzies that come from helping a student in

The $25,000 Question: Should Almost Ivy . . .

. . . give $25,000 to Monica?   or   . . . give $5,000 awards to Susan, Joe, Michael, Becky, and Jim?

	GRANT	EFC		GRANT	EFC
Monica	$25,000	$0	Susan	$5,000	$18,000
			Joe	$5,000	$17,000
			Becky	$5,000	$16,000
			Michael	$5,000	$15,000
			Jim	$5,000	$20,000

One-Year Budget Impact:
−$25,000+$0=−$25,000

Four-Year Budget Impact:
−$100,000+$0=−$100,000

One-Year Budget Impact:
−$25,000+$86,000=+$61,000

Four-Year Budget Impact:
−$100,000+$344,000=+$244,000

need. If the money goes to the other five, and all choose to enroll, the college will more than cover its $100,000 outlay by raking in $344,000 of tuition over four years. (For simplicity, we assume that any gap between the $5,000 scholarship and the EFC and the total expense will be covered by federal aid.) Of course, several of the five low-need students would probably enroll anyway. But if even one or two of them chose to come because of the $5,000 grant, the college would more than break even. An added bonus of this approach is an increase in the college's yield (the number of those accepted who actually enroll), a closely watched indicator of selectivity.

The obvious winners from the discounting game are upper-middle-class families who don't qualify for much need-based aid. They can take comfort in the fact that as tuition costs escalate, fewer and fewer students are actually paying the full price. Less than half do at most private colleges, and the figure is as low as 10 percent at schools that are heavy discounters.

And as for Monica? Every college enrolls a few like her, but most cannot afford very many. Without impeccable credentials, she is likely to get a thin letter on April 1—or a hollow acceptance, not accompanied by the aid she needs to enroll.

Some final caveats on merit and discount awards: Be sure to find out if they are renewable for four years, and if so what the requirements are. Some colleges lure students with hefty cash awards for the freshman year and then snatch some of the money away once the student is hooked. Other colleges build in sticky requirements for renewal, such as maintaining a 3.5 grade point average on a 4.0 scale.

A merit scholarship is nice recognition for hard work in high school, but never forget that it is also an enticement to buy an expensive product (albeit at a discounted price). Applicants should think hard before changing a college choice over a few thousand dollars. A discount is a good deal only if you like the merchandise.

NEED-BASED AID

It is time to lift the veil on the most complicated part of our story: the convoluted process by which colleges parcel out "need-based" aid. Need-based aid used to be the wholesome branch of financial aid in which every deserving student got all that he or she needed. But only the richest colleges can still afford the process we outlined in Financial Aid 101. Today, many colleges make admissions decisions based on who can pay, and the amount of your "need-based" aid package may depend less on your financial situation than how badly the college wants you to enroll.

One of the big problems is that few colleges are completely honest about how the system works. Like presidential candidates, they tend to speak in sound bites that mask the complexity of what they do. Applicants who want real answers must dig into the details of each college's policies.

The pages that follow examine the three most important questions facing aid applicants:

1. How does financial need affect admissions decisions?
2. How is financial need calculated?
3. How are aid packages assembled to meet the need?

Each of these questions is complicated. Many colleges, including the majority of the most selective ones, assert that financial need has no impact on admissions decisions. But even at the colleges that adhere faithfully to the policy, the phrase "need-blind admissions" is a misnomer. A glance at any applicant's file gives a strong indication of the family's financial circumstances, from information such as community of residence, zip code, high school, and parents' professions. Furthermore, communication between the admissions and financial-aid offices is ongoing throughout the process. The financial-aid office will know exactly which applicants are at the top of the list for admission (most colleges have a numerical rating system), and aid packages are constructed accordingly. The more the college wants you, the more aid you are likely to get and the higher the proportion that will come in the form of grants rather than loans.

Though no admissions office is genuinely need-blind, many choose to disregard need in making decisions. But therein lies the rub. As they ponder the fate of candidates near the admit-deny borderline, the odds of their decision are stacked against admitting the high-need students. No college wants to lavish a huge aid award on a marginal admit. Yet if these students are admitted without adequate aid, they are unlikely to enroll (thereby hurting the college's yield and selectivity rankings). Either way, the college loses.

We don't mean to suggest that all "need-blind" colleges bend the rules when confronting this dilemma. But unfortunately, some do. Need-blind policy or no, the students who squeak through in the final cut are generally the ones who can pay the freight. When considering students on the wait list, some need-blind colleges have no qualms about accepting only those with no need (rationalizing that the wait list is a special case). The colleges that are most credible in maintaining purely need-blind admissions are the ones who offer no merit scholarships. Such a policy is the best evidence of a commitment to need-based aid.

While many selective colleges are need-blind, others admit that they do consider financial need when making decisions, generally for a percentage of the decisions at the end of the process. In other words, they might admit the first 90 percent of the class on a need-blind basis, then weigh need as a factor for the last 10 percent. At Carleton College, the last 10 percent (or so) of admits are students who can pay the full bill or only need a little aid. Another prominent "need-conscious" school is Brown University, which considers need when examining 1,000 borderline candidates out of a pool of approximately 15,000 applicants. Unlike many colleges, Brown refuses to admit students whose need it cannot meet. In the words of Director of Admissions Michael Goldberger, in a recent report to secondary schools, "Brown feels strongly that we must both admit the student and provide financial assistance to attend in order to truly admit that student."

At most need-conscious schools, the rationale is less lofty. Most don't have the money to be need-blind or meet full need. At least they are honest about it. But before we give this group the Better Business Bureau seal of approval, there is one slight exaggeration we would like to point out. Any institution that says it considers need for a percentage of its decisions—say, 10 percent—actually enrolls a much higher percentage of its class that way. That's because the borderline admits chosen in need-conscious deliberations are weaker than all the other admitted students—and therefore more likely to enroll. That's one reason why need-conscious schools tend to be less diverse than genuinely need-blind ones.

DEMONSTRATED NEED AND YOUR AID PACKAGE

The impact of financial need on admissions decisions is a crucial issue, but the second half of the equation is just as important: How much of the need will be met? Only a select group of the richest colleges can afford to combine need-blind admissions with the guarantee to meet the full need of all accepted applicants.

Many colleges, need-blind or no, offer aid packages that leave a gap between the aid award and the amount a student needs to enroll. This outcome—called "gapping"—has become more widespread as college costs escalate.

Another fly in the ointment: the fact that colleges are the ones who calculate demonstrated need. A college can easily maintain the fiction of meeting full need by maintaining unreasonably high figures for loans, or by skimping on allowances for living expenses. Honest differences in methodology can also lead to wide variations in aid awards. When asking whether a college meets full need, savvy applicants should also get the lowdown on how it determines need.

Ten years ago, the process for calculating need was fairly straightforward. All colleges used the same formula for determining the Expected Family Contribution (EFC), the amount each family was required to pay for higher education. The difference between the EFC and the total expenses of attending each college was known as the demonstrated need. Though some schools occasionally tinkered with the EFC, there was general consensus on the major ground rules. Everything changed in 1992, when the Federal government decided to rewrite the financial-aid rules. It replaced the old form for calculating need with a new one, the Free Application for Federal Student Aid, which all students must file to receive aid from any college. The FAFSA examines household income and assets. After factoring in a hefty allowance for your parents' retirement nest egg (the older they are, the bigger the allowance), the formula spits out an EFC.

Though the stated goal of the FAFSA was to simplify the aid process, the behind-the-scenes explanation isn't so simple. According to one financial-aid director, the FAFSA was a power play on the part of members of Congress representing wealthy districts to change the aid formula to the benefit their constituents. In simplifying the formula, the lawmakers also hobbled its ability to ferret out the assets that affluent families are adept at hiding. Most significantly, the government eliminated home equity (the amount of money a home is worth) from the assets factored into the aid equation. That may not sound earthshaking, but the effect was to substan-

Calculating Your EFC

Listed below are approximate Expected Family Contribution figures for families of four with one child in college under the Federal Methodology (FM). (For a family with more than one child in college, the EFC is the total it is expected to spend for both.)

Expected Family Contribution as a Function of Income and Assets

		Net Assets		
	$25,000	$50,000	$100,000	$150,000
Annual income				
$20,000	0	152	1,472	2,881
$30,000	1,385	1,678	3,152	5,240
$40,000	3,037	3,423	5,646	8,466
$50,000	5,460	6,086	8,906	11,726
$60,000	8,206	8,832	11,652	14,472
$70,000	10,715	11,341	14,161	16,981
$80,000	13,655	14,281	17,101	19,921
$90,000	16,595	17,221	20,041	22,861
$100,000	19,531	20,157	22,977	25,797

The figures shown above assume that the older parent, age forty-five, is employed; the other parent is not employed; income is from employment only; no unusual circumstances; standard deduction on U.S. income tax; 1040 tax return form filed. Net assets exclude primary place of residence and family farms.

Source: College Board.

---

tially lower the EFC of aid applicants from swanky suburbs and other high-rent districts. For many colleges—especially some expensive private ones committed to meeting 100 percent of "need"—the new rules foreshadowed a severe financial hit.

While the private colleges were crying foul, the College Board entered the fray with a new supplementary financial-aid form known as the Financial Aid Profile. The primary purpose of the Profile is to provide a stan-

dardized way for expensive private colleges to put back into the formula
various factors ignored by the FAFSA. While asking many of the same
questions, the Profile goes into more detail concerning the nature of family
assets and a variety of special circumstances. Among the variables ignored
by the FAFSA but included in the Profile are:

- home equity
- trust funds held by siblings
- noncustodial parent income and assets
- medical and dental expenses
- private-school tuition
- summer earnings

In addition to the standard battery of questions, the Profile also includes
a number of "institutional questions," which are added only at the request of
each college. When students register to fill out the Profile, they must list the
colleges to which they will apply. From that list, the College Board creates
an individualized Profile for each family that includes the institutional questions required by the colleges they choose. These questions delve even
deeper into topics such as untaxed income, assets in foreign countries, business and consumer loans, and financial issues relevant to divorce. As if all

Applying for Aid: Which Forms?

FORM	REQUIRED BY
FAFSA	All colleges
Financial Aid Profile	Some expensive private colleges
College-produced form	Varies—inquire at financial aid office

that weren't enough, many colleges also require submission of their own supplemental financial aid form that asks for additional information. Despite the government's talk of simplifying the system, families now find themselves filing as many as three separate aid applications for a single college.

With such a confusing welter of forms, the task of zeroing in on how your colleges calculate need won't be easy. A good opening question might be "Do you use the Federal Methodology (FM)?" A "yes" to this question will spare you numerous headaches. You'll probably need to file only the FAFSA to qualify for aid. Most state universities use the FM, as do a number of private schools. On the downside, most FM schools do not presume to meet full demonstrated need, but instead extend an offer of admission with a "gapped" aid offer. A good question for schools in this category: Is there a standard amount of need that goes unmet?

At colleges that use their own "institutional methodology" (IM) to calculate demonstrated need, information may be harder to get. If the college requires the Profile, you can assume that all the variables in the previous discussion are included. The wealthier your family, the more likely that your EFC will be greater under FM than IM, largely because of the home-equity factor.

Among Profile schools, the biggest variable is divorce. Some schools go to great lengths to compel the noncustodial parent to pay a share of the college costs. Typical of these is Dartmouth College, which stated in a recent publication that "both natural parents have a moral obligation to cover their children's educational costs, despite any legal documents to the contrary." Though many colleges share Dartmouth's hard-line view, others are more lenient. Many women's colleges, for instance, are reluctant to reopen old wounds for single mothers by pursuing an absentee father. If your parents are divorced and financial aid will play a major role in your college choice, we recommend that you check out each college's divorce policy before you apply. A second item that bears scrutiny is the allowance for travel and living expenses that is built into demonstrated need. If a college is looking to cut corners, this is an obvious place. For schools more than a few hundred miles away, two round-trip air fares should be factored into the deal.

Though it pays to be well informed before you apply, many differences in aid policies only become apparent after the aid offers are in hand. We now turn to the various elements that make up those much-anticipated awards.

Five Good Questions for the Financial Aid Office

1. **What percentage of the last freshman class paid full tuition?** A rough indication of your odds for getting aid via merit or need.
2. **What percentage of accepted aid applicants were offered full need?** A good index of a college's aid resources and commitment to need-based aid.
3. **Is there a maximum institutional grant?** A figure that is substantially less than the college's tuition and fees will mean major-league loans for needy students.
4. **How will my aid package change after freshman year?** Most colleges will increase loans and decrease grants for upper-classmen. Find out if there are standard increments for such changes.
5. **What happens if my need increases later?** Many colleges are reluctant to raise aid amounts for students already enrolled. You'll be at their mercy then, so ask the question now.

BUILDING AN AID PACKAGE

After a college has arrived at its calculation of demonstrated need, the final piece in the puzzle is how it chooses to respond. The college will either offer a package that meets the full need, or leave the family a gap to pay (somehow) on its own. In both cases, the package will probably include aid in three varieties: grants, loans, and a work-study job. But how much of each? That is a question that bears close scrutiny.

Mix and match is the operative metaphor for financial-aid packages. Some of the money will come from the college's own funds and some will be contributed by the federal government. Loans and work-study provide the foundation of most packages. The loans might be administered by a local bank, or through the college itself, but the source of the money is much less important than how much the college chooses to give you. The loan plans come under a dizzying array of acronyms corresponding to a variety of federal and institutional programs. Many offer deferment of interest charges

The Aid Officer's Toolbox

Your financial aid officer is the point person in helping you pay for your education—like the friendly folks at car dealerships who help finance all those Chevrolets and Cadillacs. Your aid officer decides on what loans or scholarships the college is willing to offer from its own funds and serves as the coordinator of outside assistance, including federal aid and loans from private banks.

Federal money accounts for the great majority of the funds through six major programs: Pell Grants, Supplemental Educational Opportunity Grants, Perkins Loans, Stafford Loans, PLUS Loans, and Work-Study jobs. Federal loans are administered through lending instutitions, or through the colleges via the Direct Lending program. The colleges also offer grants and loans of their own and often have preferred arrangements with local banks. A number of state-sponsored grant and loan programs round out the list.

Students and parents should be less concerned with the source of their money than the bottom line: grants are free and loans must be paid back. If your aid offers include loans, check to see whether they are subsidized or unsubsidized. The former includes deferred payment and a favorable interest rate; the latter is just a regular loan that requires immediate payback. With no end in sight to the federal budget squeeze, unsubsidized loans are easily the fastest-growing form of government assistance.

Even families that do not qualify for aid may be eligible for useful financing options. Some universities will guarantee four years at the freshman-year rate if you pay the combined tuition bills at enrollment. (And in case you don't have $50,000 or $100,000 sitting around in your checking account, they will lend you the money and then let you pay it back over time.) Others negotiate loans with favorable interest rates, at local banks, that are available to all students. The Golden Rule of financial aid: Seek and ye shall find.

and flexible payment plans, but others have no deferment and no discount below the market rate.

Work-study is a federal program that subsidizes jobs for students while they attend college. Typically, the college gives the student a job in the cafeteria or an academic office, and then the wages are counted as part of his or her EFC. Most colleges generally expect students to work no more than 10 to 12 hours per week during the school year, and studies show that such a workload rarely affects student performance. One hitch: The money doesn't come in until after it is earned.

The combination of loans and work-study jobs is known in financial-aid offices as self-help. Virtually every need-based financial-aid package includes self-help, but the amount can vary widely. In the arcane world of financial-aid accounting, a $5,000 loan meets the same need as a $5,000 grant—even though the grant is for keeps and the loan must be paid back with interest. Some colleges maintain unreasonably high self-help in their aid packages to preserve the fiction of meeting "full" need while saddling students with thousands in debts. Savvy financial aid consumers will want to ask the colleges that meet full need if there is a ceiling on self-help as an aid component. A reasonable self-help limit for freshmen is approximately $6,000 per year ($4,000 in loans and $2,000 for work-study earnings). At colleges that gap, students may be loaded up with loans of thousands more. Either way, there is no substitute for comparison shopping to find out the going rate among your colleges. Another important issue is how much the self-help expectation changes in the sophomore through senior years. A $500-per-year hike in your loan component is standard practice, but be advised, as previously noted, that a few colleges will lure freshmen with generous grant aid and then put the squeeze on them with massive loans as upperclassmen.

Though loans and work-study are nice, grants are what financial aid applicants want to get their hands on. That's the real money—the kind you don't have to pay back. Once an applicant has reached the self-help limit, grant money is automatic if the college meets full need. But these days, many colleges are giving some applicants a few extra goodies in their bag of financial aid treats. More than half of four-year colleges engage in a practice called "differential packaging" or "sweetening the pot," in which certain targeted applicants are given more grants and less self-help. How likely are you to get your pot sweetened? It depends mostly on your qualifications. The admissions office will rate you against other admitted applicants, then the aid office will build a package that is more generous the higher your standing. We do, however, have one suggestion for maximizing your bargaining power: Apply to schools that compete directly with one another. When the colleges get your FAFSA report, the other schools at which you are also applying for aid appear on the printout. Some colleges will produce more generous offers if they see archrivals on the listing.

After the colleges have loaded all their stocking stuffers, the aid offers are unveiled along with the letters of acceptance (or shortly thereafter). Be prepared for wide variation in the size of your awards. Financial aid is far from an exact science, and one of the reasons applicants should apply to more than one school is the chance to compare offers.

If your awards seem too low, or your dream school offers thousands less than your safety, you and your parents should consider an appeal. With competition for students at an all-time high, many families are successful in wheedling additional dollars from the college of their choice. Rule #1: Be tactful. Begin the inquiry as an effort to understand the offer and how it was put together.

The most promising appeals are generally based on new information or special circumstances. If Grandma is in a nursing home and your parents pay part of the bill, that's a special circumstance. Ditto if your mom is laid off from her job. If Dad doesn't think the financial aid office understood the magnitude of his business debts, he should definitely call to plead his case. On the other hand, sob stories about lifestyle choices are not likely to carry much weight. If the family is strapped for cash after buying a second BMW, don't bother telling the financial-aid office.

Colleges are favorably disposed to special-circumstance appeals because those provide a rationale for changing the award. Appeals made merely to cut a better deal will encounter more resistance. Few colleges will ever publicly admit to bargaining. "We're not going to bend over backwards and award more aid to a family just because they scream louder," says Elaine Solinga of Connecticut College. The reality behind such public pronouncements will depend on the college. Some truly won't bargain, but many others are willing to up the ante—when pressed—to get a student they want.

Your best ammunition in such negotiations will be a superior offer from a competitor school. As you discuss the components of a package with Col-

---

Outside Scholarships: Can I Keep Them?

It depends. At many schools, a $3,000 scholarship from the local Rotary Club means a $3,000 reduction in aid from the colleges. Under FM, they are required to consider such awards when figuring your EFC. But the colleges have a freer hand with their own money, and some will reward your initiative by using the scholarship to replace the loan portion of your aid package rather than the grant. Some will reduce your grant, but only partially. Bottom line: Find out your college's policy on outside money.

How Much Debt Can I Afford?

Some people will pay anything to attend Dream U., but we recommend that students think twice about borrowing more than $5,000 per year. After four years at this rate, you'll pile up a debt of over $20,000 that will continue to accrue interest until you pay it back. If you try to work off a $20,000 debt in five years, you'll owe roughly $450.00 per month—about a fourth of the take-home pay of a person who earns $25,000 a year. That's no problem if you're drafted by the NFL or the NBA, but many students will want to attend graduate school and may need—you guessed it—more loans. Spreading the payments over ten years will cut your monthly bill in half, but the total you owe will also be greater because of the additional interest charges. Paying off college debt at age thirty is not an ideal situation, especially if you are trying to start a family.

lege A's financial-aid office, be sure to note which elements in College B's are more generous. If the differential will be the determining factor in your enrollment decision, make that fact clear. Few colleges can resist that kind of bait. Your bargaining power is likely to correspond to how high you rank in the pool of admitted applicants and how badly the college needs students like you. Financial-aid appeals don't always work, but there is no better way to find out if you really got the college's best offer. As long as you maintain proper courtesy, you have nothing to lose.

After all appeals have been exhausted, many unlucky souls will still find themselves gapped. If your aid offers don't meet full need, you have a decision to make. You can either attend a cheaper school or pay your way with additional loans above and beyond what the college has given you. A home-equity loan is the favored choice for many because the interest payments are generally tax-deductible. Also available is the PLUS loan program, a program for parents with no ceiling on the amount borrowed. Those who choose this option risk creating a mountain of debt. A better strategy for those who are gapped might be to work for a year between high school and college to save the much-needed funds. Most colleges will allow you to defer enrollment for a year if you want to build up your assets.

Despite all the doom and gloom surrounding financial aid in the nineties, a few bright spots are visible on the horizon. The upward spiral in college costs appears to be over, at least for the moment. Annual tuition increases, which once hovered near double digits, have settled in the 4 to 5 percent range. Many colleges are feeling the consumer backlash and are unlikely to resume steep rises. A few have even abandoned the discounting game. After years of offering discounts to 85 percent of its students, tiny Muskingum College drastically curtailed the practice while slashing tuition by almost a third. Though the number of colleges that have cut their tuition is still small, the trend bears watching for the 2000s.

19

Dave's World: A Financial Aid Time Line

To everyone who persevered through Chapter 18, we offer a hearty round of congratulations. You now know more about the financial-aid system than some people who make a living in admissions and counseling. The only thing left is to master the nuts and bolts—forms, deadlines, and all the other niggly details. To reward your persistence, we've created an applicant's helper to guide you through the maze. His name is Dave, and he's probably the most conscientious financial aid applicant who has ever lived. (You may be tempted to strangle him after a while, but remember, he's here to help you.) It will come as no surprise that Dave is one of the top students in his class. His grade point average is a sparkling 3.89, and he scored 1360 on the SAT I as a junior. Follow along with Dave's financial aid search and you won't miss a trick when it comes to your own.

Winter, Junior Year

With college looming on the horizon, Dave calls his parents together for a chat about his prospects. They're committed to paying for his college expenses, but concern in their voices is apparent from the moment he enters the room. Their incomes total $95,000 per year—too much, they fear, to qualify for the substantial financial aid they think they might need. Dave's father was recently diagnosed with Parkinson's disease, and though he still holds his job as a sales manager at a pharmaceutical company, the family is already preparing for when he will be unable to work. (He is also contemplating some experimental treatments not covered by his company's health plan.) Will the colleges make an allowance for medical expenses in their calculations? After some preliminary figuring, Dave's parents conclude that they can afford approximately $15,000 per year for his college expenses.

Both are somber as they come to the realization that some colleges may be too expensive for them to afford. "That's okay," replies Dave cheerfully. "I'll handle the rest."

Armed with the financial parameters he needs, Dave makes an appointment with his guidance counselor to officially begin the college search. Together, they settle on a two-pronged strategy that will include some schools above the $15,000 threshold and some below it. Ever since Dave read F. Scott Fitzgerald's *This Side of Paradise* as an eighth-grader, his dream has been to attend Princeton University, a school in the $25,000+ category. Several other Ivy League schools have caught his eye, as well as some elite small colleges that are highly selective and highly expensive. Dave is disappointed to learn that most of these schools do not offer merit scholarships, but his counselor suggests some other slightly less lofty selections that do. Dave knows that neither type will be possible without some form of aid, but he is determined to scrape together the money. Just in case the aid doesn't work out, Dave and his counselor also discuss a range of schools with sticker prices under $15,000. He is particularly intrigued by his counselor's list of public liberal arts colleges. Most of them don't have the big reputation of a private school, but she assures him that they provide a comparable education—often at less than half the price.

At his counselor's suggestion, Dave asks his parents to complete the financial aid estimator program on the College Board's World Wide Web site. She cautions that it will produce only a ballpark approximation of the EFCs that might be computed by particular colleges. The program is quick and easy but yields distressing news—an expected family contribution of $22,500. Without special consideration for his father's medical condition, Dave's family is unlikely to qualify for substantial need-based aid.

Spring, Junior Year

With his prospects for need-based aid looking bleaker, Dave decides to get busy on his search for scholarship money. Though he knows that colleges are

FOR PARENTS

As college approaches, transfer any savings in your child's name to your own. The aid formulas tax students' assets at a higher rate than parental ones.

the primary source for aid, they're far from the only source. A friend suggests that he look into Army ROTC, a program that will pay up to $12,000 toward his education at a number of the schools on his list in exchange for service in the reserves after college. Dave is jolted to learn that the deadline for applications is late September—barely three weeks after school starts! Though he soon decides that the army isn't for him, Dave hastily makes an appointment with his counselor to find out what other deadlines might be sneaking up on him.

Dave's counselor chuckles to find him in such a tizzy over scholarship deadlines in the spring of his junior year. She commends Dave on his conscientiousness and points him to a shelf of scholarship books and a computer workstation in the corner of the guidance office. During his free periods, he'll devote several hours to picking over those. In the meantime, Dave has a list of questions that are on his mind:

"I've heard that millions of dollars in financial-aid money goes unclaimed every year. Is that true?"

"That's just talk," his counselor replies. "I'm sure some scholarships do go unclaimed, but mainly ones targeted to specific populations. Some are for members of a particular church or for inhabitants of a particular county who belong to the Elks Club or the DAR. Sometimes private companies create scholarships for the children of their employees. The state has money set aside for war orphans. How many war orphans do you know?"

"A friend of mine got a letter from a company that guaranteed it could find ten scholarships for him for a fifty-dollar fee. It sounded like a good deal to me. What do you think?"

"I think he had better read the fine print. Most of those outfits say they'll find scholarships 'for which you qualify.' That's not to say you'll actually get them. Give me ten minutes and I'll find ten scholarships for which you qualify, too. I'll bet the scholarship database we have in the guidance office is at least as good as the one they're using. Never, ever, pay anybody to find you scholarships."

"So how do I find them on my own?"

"My rule of thumb is simple: Look local first. That's where you have the best shot at getting money. I have a file of local scholarships that you should definitely look at. Several of them even guarantee that one person from our school will win. Also check out scholarships relevant to your background and interests—your race, your religion, your parents' employers, your intended major, and so on. You can use our books and database."

"What about the World Wide Web? Is that a good place to get aid information?"

"Yes, but I don't recommend random surfing. There are too many hucksters selling information that is either useless or available free elsewhere.

Your best bet is the Financial Aid Information Page, by Mark Kantrowitz (see Chapter 7 "Where to Learn More," page 98). It includes everything you could ever want to know about financial aid, as well as links to other key aid sites and free access to FastWEB, a database of 180,000 scholarships and loans."

"Any other places to look?"

"The state has a few scholarships, though the number is dwindling. One of them is awarded on the basis of your class rank and SAT scores—I'll set it aside for you when I get the announcement. If you're really ambitious, you can try for some of the national scholarships. I receive notices for them all the time. Just remember: most get hundreds or even thousands of applicants."

"What about deadlines?"

"The deadlines vary, but some are as early as September or October. It pays to keep your eyes open and start early."

"Any other advice?"

"Don't count on finding a pot of gold. Most corporate or civil scholarships are small—in the $500 to $2,000 range. Then again, every little bit helps."

Summer Between Junior and Senior Year

Like many of his fellow applicants, Dave and his family take a summer college tour that includes many of the Eastern schools where he wants to apply. When Dave has his admissions interviews, his parents take the opportunity to meet with financial aid officials at several stops along the way. The officials are sympathetic to his father's medical problem and ask that the family outline the particulars of his condition in a letter to accompany the financial-aid application. They also suggest a letter from his physician. Though the financial-aid officers make no guarantees, Dave's parents are reassured that they will be given a fair hearing.

Fall, Senior Year

Dave returns from summer vacation with a healthy tan and a head of steam to finish out his college search. Throughout the preceding months, he has toyed with the idea of applying early decision to Princeton. But Dave was turned off by his tour guide (too "stuck up") and by the preppy aura he felt when visiting a dining hall. On a rainy day, the Gothic architecture seemed cold and forbidding. So much for Princeton. Without a clear first choice,

Dave makes peace with the fact that he will not apply early decision to any college as many of his friends are doing. From a financial-aid standpoint, his decision is a sensible one. As a potential merit scholarship candidate, his best move is to wait until all the offers are on the table before making a commitment.

As application time draws near, Dave hones his strategy for hitting financial pay dirt. All the colleges on his list reflect his preference for a small liberal arts college in or near a city. But in making his final selections, he is careful to include choices in each of three categories:

1. prestigious colleges, likely to provide the best need-based aid
2. less-selective private colleges, where he might get a merit scholarship
3. public colleges with quality programs but low tuition

In early October, Dave goes to the guidance office to get a copy of the College Board's Profile registration form. In order to register, he must designate the colleges on his list that require the Profile. In a few weeks, the College Board will send him a personalized copy of the Profile that includes the supplemental questions that each college specifies. Dave asks his parents to file it as soon as possible with income estimates for the current year. The family takes comfort in the fact that unlike the FAFSA, the Profile includes medical expenses and a place to describe special circumstances. By the end of November, the form is in the mail. In a few weeks, the College Scholarship Service will send a Data Confirmation Report re-stating the information the family submitted with instructions on how to notify the colleges of any mistakes or changes. In the event that federal processing of the FAFSA is delayed, colleges can use data from the Profile alone to make a tentative aid award.

Throughout the fall, Dave continues his search for outside scholarships. He locates a promising one for members of the Lutheran Church and files it in time for the November 15 deadline. He also finds several for students who intend to study history and another sponsored by the local Rotary Club. But

TIP To check out a college's ability to provide need-based aid, examine its endowment per student. The higher it is, the more likely the school provides generous aid packages. A typical selective private college has about $50,000 to $100,000 per student.

he also decides not to apply for several national scholarships that require long essays. Even a financial-aid whiz kid like Dave has his limits.

Winter, Senior Year

In early December, Dave's counselor announces that the FAFSA forms have arrived from the Department of Education. Dave is among the first to come to the guidance office to get one. That evening, Dave sits down with his parents to review the timetable: the form should be filed after January 1 but before the deadlines specified by the colleges. Since the earliest of the latter is February 1, the family has a one-month window at the beginning of the new year to gather its tax information and file the forms.

It will be a tight squeeze. Though Dave's parents can estimate their income from salaries and capital gains, the 1099 forms detailing the latter are yet to arrive (even after multiple phone calls to speed the process). By mid-January, they have a dilemma. They can file the FAFSA and the Profile using income estimates, or they can wait to file until after completing their tax return and risk missing a deadline. Uncertain of how to proceed, Dave calls the financial-aid office at the college with the earliest deadline. The representative advises the family to wait a few more days for the tax information, but to file the FAFSA before the deadline, based on estimated figures if necessary.

Filing with income estimates poses a slight problem because it often triggers the Verification process, in which the government requires you to submit copies of your tax forms to verify that your income estimates were accurate. If discrepancies arise, your aid award could be jeopardized. Though Verification is not as bad as getting hauled in by the IRS, it is a process to be avoided if possible. (A smaller number of applicants who file on the basis of completed tax returns are also selected for Verification.)

Fortunately, the deadline problem for Dave and his family solves itself. The final 1099 arrives on January 21, allowing them to complete the FAFSA before the deadline with an official tax return. The final element in the application process is a crucial one for Dave and his family: communication directly with the colleges. Several of them require submission of their own "institutional" form; all want copies of relevant tax documents. In addition, Dave's father has drafted a letter to each outlining his medical condition to send with a second letter from his doctor.

With all the paperwork finally out the door, Dave breathes a sigh of relief. In a few short weeks, he will receive a Student Aid Report (SAR) via return mail, calculating his EFC based on the Federal Methodology.

Tips for Filing the Profile and FAFSA

■ Make a photocopy of the form before you begin and use it for practice. Most people benefit from doing a rough draft. When filling out the real forms, always use a #2 pencil.

■ Be sure your full legal name and social security number are correct. Errors on either can cause delays in processing.

■ Fill in "0" where appropriate and never leave a question blank. Omitted questions can also lead to delays.

■ Never list money saved by the parents under student assets. Money belonging to the student is "taxed" at a much higher rate in the aid formulas.

■ If you are filling out more than one form, make sure the figures match.

■ Sign the forms and MAKE PHOTOCOPIES OF EVERYTHING. If snafus develop, you may need to send one or both directly to the colleges.

■ One month after filing each form, follow up with your colleges to make sure everything is in order.

Spring, Senior Year

Life as a second-semester senior treats Dave well. After fifteen months in the college admissions torture chamber, Dave begins to relax. The color comes back to his complexion. He goes to parties with friends on the weekends and even asks a girl from his French class to the prom.

Early April puts an extra bounce in his step when he is accepted at five of the seven colleges to which he applied. Though he does not win any of the outside scholarship competitions, Dave enjoys a menu of awards from the colleges to which he applied. Below is the list of the ones that accepted him by category, along with the all-important offers of financial aid:

Category #1: Prestigious Private Colleges

	ELITE U.	IVY U.
Sticker price:	$28,500	$29,000
Aid award:	$10,500	$5,000
Grant:	$4,500	$0
Loan:	$4,000	$3,000
Work-study:	$2,000	$2,000
Total Dave's family must pay:	$18,000	$24,000

Comments:

Though Ivy and Elite both gave Dave need-based aid, only Elite made an adjustment for his father's illness. Ivy used its standard Institutional Methodology to calculate a $24,000 Expected Family Contribution. At Elite, the financial-aid office used what is called "professional judgment" to lessen the EFC by $6,000. The issue is highly subjective, because Dave's dad is still working.

Category #2: Less-Selective Private Colleges

	ALMOST IVY U.	UP-AND-COMING U.
Sticker price:	$27,000	$26,000
Aid award:	$6,500	$21,500 Merit Award
Grant:	$5,000	
Loan:	$0	
Work study:	$1,500	
Total Dave's family must pay:	$20,500	$4,500

Comments:

Dave hit the jackpot at Up-and-Coming with a four-year, full-tuition Founder's Scholarship. He also made the final cut at Almost Ivy for a Presidential Merit Award but was nosed out by a concert violinist who is also a junior-level rodeo champion. Since he is one of Almost Ivy's strongest applicants, the university is nonetheless very interested in enrolling him. Like Elite, they have made an allowance in their need-based formula for his father's illness, though not quite as large. They also used differential packaging to substitute a $5,000 "Alumni Scholarship" for what would normally be the loan component of Dave's aid package. His combination of strong credentials and high EFC made him an ideal choice for a discount. Little did they know that their offer would be dwarfed by Up-and-Coming.

Category #3: State-Supported Liberal Arts College

PUBLIC IVY C.

Sticker Price:	$13,000
Aid award:	$0
Total cost to Dave:	$13,000

Comments:

At Public Ivy, what you see is what you get. The college offers little need-based aid and only a handful of scholarships for state residents.

Dave is one of the lucky ones. As an excellent student with relatively strong financial resources, he has avoided being gapped by any of his colleges. Not all gave the family everything it wanted, but Dave feels the satisfaction of a job well done. As icing on the cake, he wins a $500 award from the Lutheran Church scholarship contest.

Despite all the good news, his father is miffed that Ivy U. did not make a better offer. (Ivy had always been his dad's first choice.) After fretting for a week, Dave's father suggests calling to plead their case. He is sure that Ivy will beef up its package when it learns what archrival Elite has offered. Dave demurs. He has made his decision. Up-and-Coming is the school that really wants him—so that's where he'll go. The history department there is nationally known, and he liked everything about the school when he visited. As Dave sees it, the primary difference between Ivy and Up-and-Coming will be the decal in the family car's back window. For a savings of almost $80,000 across four years, that's a decal he can do without.

PART FOUR

A TIME
TO
REFLECT

20
Fat Letters and Thin

A quick glance is all you need to know if an admissions office decision letter carries tidings of great joy or cause for major depression. Meaty envelopes are stuffed with cordial letters of acceptance and information about enrollment and freshman housing. Skinny envelopes hold nothing more than a "Dear John" letter or notification that you have been placed on a wait list.

Every day your high school buzzes with gossip of who was accepted or rejected where. Your relatives keep calling to see if you've heard any news yet. The tension mounts. Your nerves become frazzled. You begin to believe your destiny will hinge on the postman's next delivery. And you're certain that if the "best" school rejects you, your life will never be the same.

Before you fling yourself off the Golden Gate Bridge, get a grip. If you've followed the advice of this book, you haven't put all your hopes and dreams into one admissions basket. There is no such thing as the perfect college, but there are scores—probably hundreds—of schools where you will fit in and get a good education. After a few weeks at your new alma mater, you'll probably forget that you ever applied anywhere else.

CAN I APPEAL A DENIAL?

In most cases, the answer is no. But if you are genuinely shocked at being denied admission, ask your counselor to call and inquire as to why. Occasionally, high school transcripts can be misinterpreted, scores lost, and so on. If the phone call yields a glimmer of hope, or if you still can't put the matter to rest, ask your counselor for the name of the admissions representative assigned to your school and write him or her a letter expressing your sincere disappointment and outlining why you still believe that this is the right school for you. Your appeal will have a better chance if you can include new information about your accomplishments or motivation. About a week after mailing the letter, call the admissions officer yourself to plead your case. No matter what his reaction, be polite. Ranting and raving from either you or your parents are guaranteed to do no good.

Though the odds of a successful appeal are about the same as winning the lottery, there are occasional success stories, such as the applicant to Wabash College who was denied admission because of his less-than-impressive academic record. This young man reapplied and asked that he be interviewed by several faculty as well as members of the admissions committee. Against all odds, he sold them in person and was admitted.

HANDLING THE WAIT LIST

Prospects for students on the wait list are brighter, though far from sunny. Along with all the acceptances and denials, most colleges put at least several hundred students on the wait list every year. Why? Because they are not sure how many of the ones they accept will actually enroll. As more and more students submit multiple applications, colleges' yields have become more unpredictable. The wait list is their margin of safety. In any particular year, most colleges take a few students from the wait list, though the number can vary widely from year to year. The odds of any individual student being accepted from a wait list are less than 50/50 but by no means minuscule.

If you find yourself on a wait list, your first move should be to send a deposit to your first choice among the colleges that accepted you. You don't need to tell this college that you are pursuing the wait list somewhere else; all of them know that a percentage of those who say yes in April will end up elsewhere in September.

Next, think hard about whether pursuing the wait list is worth the time, effort, and agony. Though most wait-list activity occurs by the end of May, sometimes applicants are left dangling throughout the summer. Even if you hang in there and do everything right, success is far from assured.

The wait list is an all-or-nothing proposition. To give yourself a chance, you'll need to mount a well-orchestrated campaign, enlisting the support of your teachers and counselors. "Calculated persistence and repeated statements of interest can pay off," says David Erdmann of Rollins College. "Don't be afraid to show your stuff."

To begin, fill out the postcard to express interest in pursuing the wait list and send it in. Next, consider doing some or all of the following:

- Send a letter ASAP to the admissions director emphasizing your unyielding desire to attend. State specifically why you think the match is a good one, and highlight new information.
- Call to see if you can arrange a campus interview. "Students who have been offered regular admission wait-list status are well advised to pay a visit by mid-April, perhaps with a set of recent grades in hand!" says Peter Van Buskirk of Franklin and Marshall.
- Send examples of impressive work. This is particularly relevant if you have an area of special talent, or if you have produced new work of which you are especially proud.
- Ask a current teacher to write a recommendation highlighting your recent achievements. Ask teachers who wrote letters for you previously to send updates.
- Ask your guidance counselor to write or call, and see that the admissions office is kept up to date with your grades and other achievements.

Unfortunately, ability to pay also intrudes into the wait-list process. Most colleges have little or no financial aid remaining when they get to the wait list, and as a result, high-need students rarely make it. Those with little or no need have the best chance, and your chances will improve if you can assure the college that you plan to attend with or without aid.

Through it all, be a model of politeness. If you get testy or try to use pressure tactics, the game is over. Colleges use spots on the wait list to make dreams come true for a lucky handful who have clearly communicated their wishes.

ON THE MEANING OF A COLLEGE EDUCATION

Contrary to what many people would have you believe, deciding which college to attend is not the most important decision you will ever make. Not even close. Though it makes sense to choose a college carefully, the really important stuff goes on after you enroll.

Abraham Lincoln was once riding through New Jersey on a train that passed by Rutgers College. He looked out the window and remarked, "One of my greatest regrets of my life is that I did not receive a college education." The real value of college lies in what it does for you as a person—in expanding your horizons, challenging your beliefs, honing your skills, and exposing you to the broadest possible cross section of people and ideas.

Today's world is competitive, and many high school students seem to believe that only students from certain "name" colleges will be successful. The fact is, there are plenty of students who didn't go to Prestige U.—for whatever reason—who will rise just as high and reach just as far as any who did. When the story of your lifetime is told, the name of your college will be little more than a footnote. Success will come because of who you are, not what college you attended.

21
Some Thoughts for Parents

Being the parent of a college applicant is a white-knuckle experience. Like the basketball coach who sits helplessly as his team launches a last-second shot, parents can do little more than cheer from the sidelines as their child aims for Dream U. As many parents know from experience, the pressure of the big game is often more intense for those who watch than those who play.

Basketball analogies aside, there *are* things parents can do to help assure a successful college search. This chapter will cover a number of them, but one stands out: the ability to maintain perspective. Parents have seen more of life than their children: they've wept tears of joy in hospital delivery rooms and tears of sorrow beside open caskets. When college admission begins to seem like life or death in the eyes of a seventeen-year-old, parents must be there to help restore perspective.

Different applicants have different needs. Some students need a nudge to get motivated, others need reassurance to avoid paralyzing fear. Some need encouragement to aim higher, others need to know that attending a less-prestigious school doesn't make them a lesser person. Many applicants simply need space to explore. You know your child better than anyone; try to maintain enough perspective to provide what he or she needs.

The task is by no means easy. Psychologists know that major separation events can cause dysfunctional behaviors. One of the most common is denial. If your son or daughter has trouble focusing on the college search—or actively refuses to think about it—the reason may not be indifference. Many students use such tactics to avoid confronting a reality that scares them. If your student is in denial, stay calm. When students drag their feet, parents often feel an exaggerated sense of urgency. Resist the temptation to deliver ultimatums—or worse, take over the college search yourself. Such overreactions cause resentment and reinforce your child's dependence.

Instead, help your child get unstuck with steady encouragement. For those with patience, the college search usually has a way of working out.

As graduation and college decision time draw near, many families experience an upsurge in conflict. The approach of college often intensifies arguments about curfews and duties. Students act out resentment toward parents, who in turn may show a heightened desire to "hang on" or seize a last chance to impart wisdom or values. If you feel such a spiral coming on, help your child take a step back. The amount of familial conflict at this time of life is often proportional to the amount of love.

Amid all the tumult, good parents will constantly seek ways to move the process forward. Here are some tips:

COMMUNICATE

One of the most important things that parents can do is encourage their sons and daughters to think through the basic questions. Why do you want to go to college? What are your most important needs and goals? What kind of college will best serve them? Communicating with an adolescent is not always easy, but look for the moments that present themselves. Being available to talk when your child has a question or wants to express an idea or feeling is one of the most important things you can do.

SET FINANCIAL PARAMETERS

Paying for college is the area where parents have veto power. Try to reach an understanding early in the process as to how much each party is expected to pay (before hopes get pinned on a college that may be financially out of reach). If you haven't already done so, read the two chapters on financial aid. Then sit down with your child to formulate guidelines for the search.

BE REALISTIC

Don't set your child up for failure by encouraging unrealistic applications. Look honestly at your child's academic record. Then study the admissions profiles of the colleges that show up on your lists. If he or she is not Stanford material, don't swing by Palo Alto on your college tour. Make it your task to be sure that your son or daughter applies to at least two colleges where he or she will definitely be accepted. Then even the worst-case scenario will still result in a productive college career.

THINK BROADLY

The United States has the best and most diverse system of higher education anywhere in the world. As we've said many times, there are scores of colleges that would be a good match for every student. You are probably in a better position than your son or daughter to understand this and help discourage fixation on a single "dream" school (that may be highly selective). Some of the best colleges for your child may be ones that neither of you has ever heard of.

LET THE STUDENT TAKE CENTER STAGE

In the college search, nothing is worse than a parent who steals the spotlight. Many parents, especially successful ones, are accustomed to manipulating the system to make it work for them. Resist the temptation. The admissions process is the time for teenagers to stand on their own. Parental attempts at "marketing" or influence peddling often do more harm than good.

DON'T LIVE THROUGH YOUR CHILD

Many parents subconsciously relive their own hopes and dreams through their children. Some want children to follow in their footsteps, others want them to achieve things that they themselves never could. Still other parents see college admissions as their shot at an A+ in parenting. Having hopes for your children is natural, but try to spare them the burden of expectations. One of the greatest gifts you can give your child is the freedom to follow his or her own dreams.

BE SUPPORTIVE

As the process unfolds, remind your children that they will be accepted at a good school—one where they will make friends, have fun, be challenged, and get the education they deserve. When the decisions come in, redouble your efforts on this score, and if necessary, remind them of the fickle nature of the whole selection process.

We close with a message to parents delivered by the counselors at Weston High School in Connecticut. Though written many years ago, the sentiments are as timely now as the day they were written: "We should help [our children] understand that we love and care for them no matter what a given college decides," they wrote. "We need to make it clear to them that college admission decisions are *not* evaluations of them either as students or as valuable human beings. Let them know that no matter what, you believe they are unique individuals whom you love and respect."

APPENDIX
What to Do When

SOPHOMORE YEAR

Take challenging courses and make plans for honors and/or AP work in grades eleven and twelve. Take the PSAT in October if offered for sophomores at your school. Advanced students should consider taking SAT II subject tests in May or June.

JUNIOR YEAR

Keep working hard! Your chances for admission or a scholarship will depend largely on your academic record.

September–November

Begin sizing up your college needs. Read college guides and/or use a computer college search. Meet with guidance counselor. Take the PSAT.

December–February

Consider an SAT prep course and register for the January, March, and/or May administration of the SAT I. Register for ACT if applicable. Talk to parents, teachers, older friends, and guidance counselors about colleges. Discuss finances and the college-selection process with parents.

March–April

Sift through college mail. Begin preliminary winnowing. Meet with your guidance counselor to discuss a preliminary list of twenty to thirty colleges. Begin visiting colleges and/or plan summer visits. Take the SAT I or ACT if scheduled. Register for June administration of SAT IIs.

May

Settle on a working list of 10 to 12 colleges and continue scheduling visits. Take SAT I and SAT II tests if scheduled.

June

Take SAT IIs or ACT if scheduled. Relax and enjoy the end of school.

July–August

Go on summer visits. Drop schools from your list and add others. Talk to friends about colleges they are interested in. Begin work on college essays. Prepare for fall standardized tests.

SENIOR YEAR

September

Continue college visits. Meet with your counselor. Consider early decision or early action. Get application forms from the colleges. Arrange to take the SAT I and II and ACT in October, November, and December. Continue scholarship search throughout the year.

October

Continue college visits, file early decision/action applications if applicable. Settle on final list of five to seven schools to apply to. Get a copy of your transcript and check it over. Talk with your counselor about the logistics of the application process. Ask teachers to write recommendations and provide them with the necessary forms and envelopes. Double-check deadlines for admission, housing, and financial aid. If applying to selective private colleges, register to receive the College Board Financial Aid Profile form. If applying for early decision/action, file as soon as possible. Take SAT I or II or ACT if scheduled. (Last date for first round early decision/action.)

November

File applications with December deadlines. Continue distributing recommendation forms. Continue working on applications. Take SAT I or II if scheduled.

December

File applications with January deadlines. Politely check with teachers and counselor to make sure that recommendations and transcript have been sent. Get free Application for Federal Student Aid (FAFSA) from the guidance office or the World Wide Web and ask parents to begin collecting tax information. Take SAT I or II or ACT. (Last date for January or February deadlines.)

January–February

Continue to file applications. Call admissions offices to verify that your applications are complete. File the FAFSA and Profile forms and be ready for follow-up. Take final SAT I or II or ACT.

March–April

Receive decision letters. Scrutinize financial aid offers and call the colleges if you have concerns. If you are wait listed, follow up with a letter and additional recommendations. Schedule last-minute visits to colleges where accepted or wait listed. Make final decision and send in deposit.

May

Take SAT II tests. Give yourself a pat on the back. You did it!

ACKNOWLEDGMENTS

We are grateful to many people for help in the preparation of this book. First and foremost, we would like to thank the scores of college admissions and financial-aid professionals who gave us an inside look at how the system really works. We are particularly grateful to those who offered comments on portions of the manuscript, including Valerie R. Bell, Wynne Curry, Pam Fay-Williams, Donald J. Heider, Betsy Hughes, Whitney Lloyd, Gary Sabourin, and Susan Sour. We are deeply indebted to David Miller, Director of Financial Aid at the College of Wooster, for his help in navigating the labyrinth of college financial aid. Julie Fiske Hogan stepped in with efficiency and good cheer to help verify quotes and check facts. The efforts of all are much appreciated, but responsibility for the final product is ours alone.

ONE-HOUR COLLEGE
FINDER INDEX

Note: This index includes all the institutions in the One-Hour College Finder. Institutions marked with an asterisk are the subjects of in-depth articles in *The Fiske Guide to Colleges*.

Juilliard School: dance, 94; drama, 93; music, 92

K

*Kalamazoo College: innovative, 76; international studies, 77; study abroad, 78
*Kansas, University of: architecture, 85; film/television, 97
*Kenyon College: art and design, 90; dance, 94; drama, 93; top colleges, 45
*Knox College: best-kept secrets, 60

L

*Lafayette College: engineering, 84; small colleges, 54
*Lake Forest College: art and design, 90; small colleges, 54
Landmark College: learning disabilities, 79
*Lawrence University: drama, 93; music, 92; small colleges, 55
*Lehigh University: architecture, 85; business, 88; engineering, 84; well-known universities, 58
*Lewis and Clark College: business, 88; international studies, 77; nonconformist, 74; small colleges, 55; study abroad, 78
Lincoln University (Pennsylvania): black institutions, 65
Loras College: learning disabilities, 79
Loyola University: music, 92
Lynn University: learning disabilities, 79

M

*Macalester College: drama, 93; top colleges, 45
Manhattan School of Music, 92
*Manhattanville College: art and design, 90; music, 92
Marist College: learning disabilities, 79
*Marlboro College: nonconformist, 73
*Marquette University: Roman Catholic world, 68
Maryland Institute, College of Art: art and design, 89
*Mary Washington College: small-college bargains, 50
*Massachusetts, University of/Amherst:

international studies, 77; well-known universities, 58
Massachusetts College of Art: art and design, 89
*Massachusetts Institute of Technology: architecture, 85; business, 87; elite, 39; top technical, 83
Memphis State University: film/television, 97
Mercyhurst College: learning disabilities, 79
*Miami, University of (Florida): music, 92
*Miami University (Ohio): architecture, 86; budget ivy league, 47; business, 88
*Michigan, University of: architecture, 86; art and design, 90; business, 88; communications/journalism, 95; engineering, 83; film/television, 97; honors programs, 51; music, 92; well-known universities, 58
*Michigan State University: engineering, 83
*Middlebury College: environmental studies, 76; international studies, 77; rising stars, 42; study abroad, 78
*Millsaps College: best-kept secrets, 60
*Mills College: music, 92; women's colleges, 63
*Minnesota, University of/Morris: small-college bargains, 50
*Minnesota, University of/Twin Cities: budget ivy league, 47
*Missouri, University of/Columbia: communications/journalism, 96
Mitchell College: learning disabilities, 80
Moore College of Art and Design, 90
*Morehouse College: black institutions, 65–66; business, 88; small-college bargains, 51
Morgan State University: black institutions, 66
*Mount Holyoke College: women's colleges, 63
Muskingum College: learning disabilities, 80

N

*Nebraska, University of/Lincoln: music, 92
*New College of the University of South Florida: small-college bargains, 50
New England Conservatory of Music, 92
New England, University of: learning disabilities, 80

Tuskegee University: black institutions, 66; engineering, 84

U

*Union College: engineering, 84; small colleges, 56

V

*Vanderbilt University: conservative, 72; engineering, 83; rising stars, 43
*Vassar College: drama, 93; small colleges, 56
*Vermont, University of: business, 88; environmental studies, 77; learning disabilities, 79; well-known universities, 59
*Villanova University: Roman Catholic world, 68–69
*Virginia, University of: budget ivy league, 48; business, 88; honors programs, 52; learning disabilities, 79; rising stars, 43
*Virginia Polytechnic Institute and State University (Virginia Tech): architecture, 86; engineering, 84
Visual Arts, School of: art and design, 90; film/television, 97

W

*Wabash College: conservative, 71
*Wake Forest University: business, 87; rising stars, 43
*Washington, University of: architecture, 86; art and design, 90; budget ivy league, 48; drama, 93; engineering, 84; environmental studies, 77
*Washington and Lee University: business, 88; conservative, 72; small colleges, 56
*Washington University (Missouri): architecture, 85; art and design, 90;

business, 87; dance, 94; engineering, 83; top colleges, 45
Wayne State University: film/television, 97
*Wellesley College: architecture, 86; elite, 41; women's colleges, 64
*Wells College: women's colleges, 64
*Wesleyan University: elite, 41; music, 93
Westminster College (Missouri): learning disabilities, 80
West Virginia Wesleyan College: learning disabilities, 80
*Wheaton College (Illinois): conservative, 71; music, 93
*Wheaton College (Massachusetts): small colleges, 56
*Whitman College: best-kept secrets, 61
*Willamette University: best-kept secrets, 61
*William and Mary, College of: budget ivy league, 49; business, 88; international studies, 77
*Williams College: art and design, 90; elite, 41–42
*William Smith College: small colleges, 54
*Wisconsin, University of/Madison: budget ivy league, 49
*Wittenberg University: best-kept secrets, 61
*Wofford College: small colleges, 56
*Wooster, College of: small colleges, 57
*Worcester Polytechnic Institute: top technical, 83

X

*Xavier University (Louisiana): black institutions, 66; Roman Catholic world, 69

Y

*Yale University: architecture, 86; drama, 93; elite, 40; music, 92

GENERAL INDEX

228

ABOUT THE AUTHORS

In 1980, when he was education editor of *The New York Times*, **Edward B. Fiske** sensed that college-bound students and their families needed better information on which to base their educational choices. Thus was born *The Fiske Guide to Colleges* (Times Books), which quickly established itself as the most authoritive guidebook of its type. A graduate of Wesleyan University, Fiske did graduate work at Columbia and assorted other bastions of higher learning. He left *The Times* in 1991 to pursue a variety of educational and journalistic interests, including a major book on school reform entitled *Smart Schools, Smart Kids* (Simon & Schuster). When not visiting colleges, he can often be found playing squash, sailing, or doing research on the educational problems of Third World countries. A resident of New Hampshire, Fiske is a director of the American Association for Higher Education and a member of the nominating panel for the Charles A. Dana Awards for Pioneering Achievements in Education.

Since getting into Yale in the early 1980s, **Bruce G. Hammond** has devoted much of his time to counseling others on college admissions. At Yale, Hammond was editor in chief of *The Insider's Guide to the Colleges*. He subsequently served as managing editor of three editions of *The Fiske Guide to Colleges*. He is now director of college counseling at Lake Ridge Academy in Cleveland, where he also teaches the finer points of AP U.S. history to a group of intelligent but sleep-deprived eleventh- and twelfth-graders.